MW00579599

ENTHUSIASM

Cultural Memory
in
the
Present

Mieke Bal and Hent de Vries, Editors

ENTHUSIASM

The Kantian Critique of History

Jean-François Lyotard

Translated by Georges Van Den Abbeele

STANFORD UNIVERSITY PRESS

STANFORD, CALIFORNIA

2009

Stanford University Press
Stanford, California

Enthusiasm: The Kantian Critique of History was originally published in French in 1986 under the title *L'enthousiasme, La critique kantienne de l'historie* © 1986, Editions Galilée.

This book has been published with the assistance of the French Ministry of Culture—National Center for the Book.

Printed in the United States of America on acid-free, archival-quality paper.

Library of Congress Cataloging-in-Publication Data

Lyotard, Jean-François, 1924–1998.
   [Enthousiasme. English]
   Enthusiasm : the Kantian critique of history / Jean-François Lyotard, Georges Van Den Abbeele.
      p. cm.—(Cultural memory in the present)
   "[O]riginally published in French in 1986 under the title L'enthousiasme, la critique kantienne de l'histoire."
   Includes bibliographical references.
   ISBN 978-0-8047-3897-2 (cloth : alk. paper)
   ISBN 978-0-8047-3899-6 (pbk. : alk. paper)
   1. History—Philosophy—History—18th century. 2. Kant, Immanuel, 1724–1804. I. Van Den Abbeele, Georges. II. Title. III. Series.
D16.7.L95   2009
901—dc22

2008043114

Contents

Translator's Preface

As Jean-François Lyotard indicates, *Enthusiasm* was first read as a paper in May 1981 at an ongoing seminar held at the Ecole Normale Supérieure (ENS) in Paris, hosted by Jean-Luc Nancy and Philippe Lacoue-Labarthe under the provocative moniker, Centre de recherches philosophiques sur le politique (Center for Philosophical Research on the Political).

Although brief and written as a philosophically technical reading of Kant, *Enthusiasm* also marks the full transition from Lyotard's earlier Freudo-Marxist preoccupation with libidinal politics and cultural revolution to his latter work on more discursive models of social justice and ethics, as evidenced in *The Differend* (1983) and ensuing texts. His involvement in the ENS seminar represents his convergence with a general reevaluation of political thought spanning a number of leading French intellectuals, from renegades of the French Communist Party (PCF) like Etienne Balibar seeking an alternative to what appeared to be an increasingly out-of-touch Marxist orthodoxy, to Derrideans seeking a more overt political engagement for the philosophical practice of deconstruction, to *nouveaux philosophes* like Luc Ferry looking for a return to liberal-republican political principles. Common among this striking breadth of thinkers and what brought them together for the life of the ENS center (roughly 1980–84) was a strong sense of the futility and/ or limitations of politics per se in the strict sense of the word ("*la* politique," as the French say) as an agent of change and social betterment. A combination of factors fueled this sentiment: the aspirations of May 1968 receding into the horizon of history after a frustrating decade of conservative rule and electoral domination, accompanied by an increasing skepticism toward the traditional parties of the Left to deliver anything *"l'alternance"*

more than a narrow, predictable agenda, and a nascent postmodernist sense of politics as a fundamentally mediatic phenomenon (viz. the so-called spectator society). Real politics, being political (in the French sense of "*le* politique") was to be found elsewhere, in the workings of daily life, in education, in cultural production, in the rise of alternative institutions and identity-based organizations. In short, these intellectuals were living through the worldwide crisis of the new Left, an intellectually energizing crisis if we consider some of the later production by such thinkers, who briefly saw common cause, or at least a common venue, in a theoretical moment that would generate what would come to be called post-Marxism. Jean-Luc Nancy's *The Inoperative Community* (1986) and *The Experience of Freedom* (1988); Etienne Balibar's *Race, Nation, Class* (with Immanuel Wallerstein; 1988), and the essays gathered in *Masses, Classes, Ideas* (1994); as well as Jacques Derrida's *Specters of Marx* (1993) and Lyotard's *The Differend* can all be seen to derive from these seminar discussions at the ENS in the early eighties. It is, of course, somewhat ironic that this intellectual activity spawned by a sense of electoral defeat and skepticism should itself have occurred during the months leading right up to and following the dramatic socialist victory in May 1981 that propelled François Mitterrand to the presidency, thus making real the vaunted Gaullist principle of "l'alternance" whereby Right and Left could be in power one after the other without disrupting the fundamental continuity of the Fifth Republic. Disbelief at the prospect of socialist victory, however, soon passed into cynicism over the impracticality of realizing the utopic dreams still held by the "soixante-huitards," and the socialist government's concomitant sense of being abandoned by the intelligentsia.[1]

Where does Lyotard fit into this scenario? For him, the work that issued forth in *Enthusiasm* was not a foray into some new post-Marxist experiment but in fact the end of a long theoretical trek that began with his experiences up close with the Algerian revolution and his work in the 1950s for the revisionist left-wing journal *Socialisme ou barbarie?* and continued up through his experience as a professor at Nanterre during the beginnings of the May 1968 disturbances. Lyotard was not discovering post-Marxism but in fact emblematized an old form of post-, or rather one should call it, revisionist Marxism, one steeped in the old

descriptive vs prescriptive

Second International debates about spontaneism (Rosa Luxemburg) and council communism (Antonie Pannekoek), and characterized by a deep suspicion about the kind of party vanguardism and bureaucratic rule that would characterize Marxist-Leninism and Soviet communism. For Lyotard, the perceived failures of the FLN in Algeria to represent and champion grassroots resistance to French rule were mirrored by the perceived hostility/incomprehension of the communist leadership toward the student demonstrations in 1968, in both cases exemplifying the insensitivity of party leadership to broader cases of injustice and disaffected groups (viz. young people, women, minorities, and so forth).

Questions of distributive justice and the politics of representation thus preoccupy Lyotard throughout the late 1970s and ultimately motivate his abandoning Freud for Wittgenstein, the expressiveness of repressed desire for the matrix of language games. In *Au juste*, published in 1979 and very much written under the tenseness of the left-wing terrorism that then wracked western Europe (Baader-Meinhof in Germany, the Red Brigades in Italy, along with their imitators and admirers), Lyotard attempts to develop an ethics of political and theoretical engagement based on the discursive distinction between descriptive and prescriptive utterances and on the logical, and indeed moral, falseness of deriving one from the other.

Enthusiasm takes this "philosophy of phrases," as Lyotard would come to call it, and maps it onto the Kantian "faculties," in the process rethinking and repurposing what are psychological/cognitive categories in the philosophy of Kant (understanding, reason, imagination, and so on) into discursive units he terms "phrases," such as interrogatives, cognitives, imperatives, and so forth. Two remarks are in order here. First, Lyotard's revisionist reading of Kant has been influential in proposing post-Marxist alternatives to classic Hegelian Marxism, as if the desire to move beyond Hegel involved a stepping back *before* Hegel, back to Kant. More to the point, by moving beyond the traditional phenomenological worrying over the "ding-an-sich" and focusing on the complex architectonics of the Kantian project as a way to think through issues of difference and justice, Lyotard is able to theorize dissonant forms of ethical and political activism beyond the politics of consensus and representation. The reputedly static antithetic and dialectic of Kant thus allow the theorization of nontraditional models of dissent (or "dissensus," as Lyotard liked to say) and unpresentable cases of injustice (eventually, his notion of the "differend").

The second remark concerns the use of the word *phrase*, normally translated into English as "sentence." Like a sentence, a *phrase* is a unit of communication, and elsewhere, Lyotard breaks it down into a pragmatic interface (between one or more interlocutors, reference, and meaning). It is this pragmatic dimension that becomes Lyotard's focus, exceeding any limitation to language narrowly understood (in *The Differend* he gives the movement of a cat's tail as meeting the criterion for a "phrase"). It is also what propels him to focus less on what is happening in any given "phrase" than in the interrelations between "phrases," or "phrasing" (and this verbal dimension further motivates the translation of the word by its English cognate).

How to "phrase," or move judiciously from one phrase to the next, is the core of Lyotard's project and one that urges his close attention to Kant's "third" *Critique*, that of the power of judgment. The so-called faculty of judgment in Kant is not a "faculty" at all but the power (*kraft*) that articulates the relation between faculties. Just as the third *Critique* seeks the "passage" between the first two *Critique*s, that is, between the *Critique of Pure Reason* and the *Critique of Practical Reason*—between the understanding (cognition) and moral imperative, between the laws of nature and the prerogative of freedom, between what is and what ought to be—so the judgment seeks passageways between phrases. This makes the judgment a *critical* (both discriminating and evaluating) activity—an *urteilskraft*—and, as critique, it speaks to the heart of the philosophical enterprise. To the extent, though, that judgment as a critical articulation of phrases engages both temporality and causality, it becomes, as Lyotard argues in the first chapter of this book, an analog for the historical and the political. Judgment becomes a kind of navigating between phrases in an archipelago of discursive (and political) possibilities. The exploration of that archipelago would be the material for a "fourth" critique, a critique of the historical and political. Such a critique was, of course, never written by Kant, but something like a "critique of historico-political reasoning" can be retrieved out of the scattered, short works Kant produced near the end of his life on topics such as "Idea

Enthusiase vs Schwärmerie

for a Universal History from a Cosmopolitan Point of View" (1784); "Answer to the Question: What Is Enlightenment?" (1784); "Conjectural Beginning of Human History" (1786); "Perpetual Peace" (1795); or *The Conflict of the Faculties* (1798).

In a sense, such a Kantian critique of history continues the work of the *Critique of Judgment*, not only in terms of the latter's analytic of teleological judgment (or purposiveness) but more crucially that of the analytic of aesthetic judgment, and even more specifically that of the analytic of the sublime. If, as Kant argues, the judgment of beauty occurs because of a harmonious interaction between faculties, the sublime proposes precisely a gap, a disharmony between faculties, an irreconcilability that cannot be translated, that is "incommensurable." It is the incommensurability between faculties (or phrases) that intrigues Lyotard and where he finds the ground zero of history and politics.

For Lyotard, the feeling of the sublime is therefore as political as it is aesthetic, and it comes to the fore especially in those historical moments that do not follow the scripting of what Lyotard elsewhere calls "grand narratives" (such as the dialectics of class struggle, the march of liberal democracy, the progress of technology, Christian eschatology, and so on). Such unsuspected and unpredictable "events" open up or deliver (*Begebenheit*) the potential for vastly different political/historical outcomes. Such a *Begebenheit* thus reveals an incommensurability between phrases, whence the sublime. "Enthusiasm" would be a "strong" sense of the sublime, for which Kant gives the example of the popular response to the French Revolution, that is, a widespread or "common" expression of hopefulness toward a political reality better and different than the autocratic rule of feudal kings and princes. Such "enthusiasm" for the French Revolution was, of course, itself a risky expression in other countries, yet it is precisely that danger and its overcoming that qualify the sublimity of that feeling as enthusiasm and not merely the "tumultuousness of exaltation [*Schwärmerei*]." What Lyotard finds especially intriguing in this Kantian notion of enthusiasm is that it involves not the great actors or participants in the historical events of the revolution but rather the response (or judgment) of the *spectators* of those events, however far away, as a form of political engagement through their recognition of the *Begebenheit* as a "sign of history."

The contemporary enthusiasm of people around the world for the French Revolution is not a mere historical curiosity for Lyotard, but the very crux of a political thinking that highlights events such as those of May 1968 in France, Hungary in 1956, or Czechoslovakia in 1968, or Gdansk in 1970 and 1980. Lyotard could not, of course, have cited the later popular uprisings that would sweep through Eastern Europe in 1989, some eight years after he wrote *Enthusiasm*, and yet this work uncannily foresees and theorizes such unexpected and unscripted events—even the risks incurred in the manifestation of such enthusiasm, if we recall how the popular expression in China of "enthusiasm" for the events in Eastern Europe was countered by the massacre at Tiananmen Square.

As such, this short work by Jean-François Lyotard remains a powerful way to think through such sudden historical/political change not just as nostalgia for past revolutionary action but as the spontaneous work of popular expression, the sublime as a *sensus communis*, with necessarily unpredictable results. The analysis still obtains in our post–cold war, neoliberal world order with its media-saturated environment and an increasingly interactive technology (such as the Internet) that allows for ever-more unforeseeable and unscriptable moments of "enthusiasm."

6/23/09

Notice

This study served as the basis for a talk I gave on April 27, 1981, at the Center for Philosophical Research on the Political, which was instituted at the Ecole Normale Supérieure in the rue d'Ulm [Paris—Trans.] on the initiative of Philippe Lacoue-Labarthe and Jean-Luc Nancy in November 1980 and suspended by them in November 1984.[1]

A portion of the study was published under the title "Introduction à une étude du politique selon Kant," in the first volume of the Center's publications, entitled *Rejouer le politique* (Paris: Galilée, 1981), along with studies by Etienne Balibar, Luc Ferry, Philippe Lacoue-Labarthe, and Jean-Luc Nancy.[2] Another version, also abridged, was made available in *Recherches sur la philosophie et le langage* (Grenoble: Presses universitaires de Grenoble, 1983) under the title "L'archipel et le signe (sur la pensée kantienne de l'historico-politique)."[3] Finally, one can find bits of this study resurfacing in *The Differend*, especially in the "Kant Notices."[4]

As for the current edition, the only one that is complete, the initial text has been entirely revised, though in conformity with the spirit that guided it when I wrote it, during 1980–81, while preparing *The Differend*.

The Center's rules required the talk's author to circulate to participants, several weeks before the meeting, an "argument" sketching out what he would say. The announcement for my study is reproduced here in the guise of an "abstract."

Allusions to talks and discussions that had previously taken place at the Center will be found, here and there, in the "argument" and in the course of the study. In particular, the first part of the study consists in a refutation of one aspect of the arguments Luc Ferry raised against Jean-Luc Nancy's talk on the Hegelian monarch. Ferry maintained that the only correct method for reading a philosophical text (that of Hegel, in this instance) was to stick strictly to internal criticism. The text of the "Opening Address," delivered by Philippe Lacoue-Labarthe and Jean-Luc Nancy, and Nancy's Hegel talk can be found in the volume *Rejouer le politique.* Unfortunately, the discussion in question was not reproduced there.[5]

I thank Christine Pries for the help she gave me in editing this text.

June 1986

Argument

1. We will be referring to the Kantian texts concerning the politico-historical while setting aside the doctrine of right. Why? There is an affinity between the critical (the "tribunal" of critique, the "judge" who examines the validity of the claims of various phrase families—the expression here is deliberately Wittgensteinian) and the politico-historical: each has to make judgments without having a rule for making judgments, as opposed to the politico-juridical (which in principle has the rule of right). To say it otherwise: just as the critical, in Kant, should not lend itself to doctrine (but to critique), so there ought not to be a doctrine of the politico-historical. Perhaps even more than that of an affinity, their relation is that of an analogy: perhaps the critical (still in the Kantian sense) is the political in the universe of philosophical phrases, and perhaps the political is the critical (in the Kantian sense) in the universe of sociohistorical phrases.

2. The critical is determined in general as reflective. It does not arise from a faculty, but from a quasi- or "as-if" faculty (the faculty of judging, sentiment) inasmuch as its rule for determining which universes are pertinent to it entails some indeterminacy (the free play of the faculties among themselves). It decides on the legitimacy of the respective claims (to meaning) of each phrase family (called "faculty") over its family of phrase universes ("object" for Kant, but also addressee in the second and third *Critiques*). It decisively divides [*tranche*], thus revealing the incommensurability between different phrase families (of experience, of science, of Ideas, of practice). But it also "mediates" ["*transige*"][1] and is able not only to recognize legitimacies local to each phrase family but also to suggest "passages" between object regions subjected respectively to rules that are nonetheless "heterogeneous." An inventory of several words

designating these "passages": example, schema, symbol, type, Ideal of reason, Ideal of sensibility or monogram, *signum historicum* . . .

3. We will take a census of the different phrase families at play in presentations of the politico-historical: descriptive (experience), explicatory (understanding), dialectical (the Idea of speculative and/or practical reason), deontic (the regulative Idea of the practical imperative: "all rational beings"), teleological (the Idea of the purposiveness [*finalité*] of nature within man: progress), fictional (the Idea of the imagination: stories of origins, stories of ends). Kant himself (?) generally writes reflectively (= as a critic) about the politico-historical: he determines the legitimacy of these various phrases that present this universe, and he suggests possible transactions between them, that is to say, "passages": signs of all sorts, thanks to which is reestablished a unity of the politico-historical, though an undetermined one. It thus happens that his text (his concatenation of phrases) itself obeys the rules of this or that phrase family. And finally, no matter what the phrase family "chosen," these writings are themselves presented as contributions to the effectuation of the politico-historical (the role of philosophers, the necessity of the *Oeffentlichkeit* [public space]): thus immanent to the universe they present.

4. Within this problematic, the "retreat" of politics (the Center's inaugural theme) would be the retreat of the vain pretense of any given phrase family to present in and of itself the entirety of the political; hence, the retreat of political doctrine per se, of whatever kind. This retreat is constantly effaced by the demand for a well-regulated singleness [*unicité*], a demand fed by horror or anxiety before incommensurability (baptized as the destruction of the social bond, or "delegitimation"). Philosophy of the political, that is, "free" reflections or critique concerning the political, shows itself to be political by discriminating between the heterogeneous phrase families that present the political universe and by following out the "passages" (the "guiding thread," writes Kant) that are indicated between them (for example, is the "enthusiasm" of 1968 like what Kant analyzes for that of 1789?).

ENTHUSIASM

The Critical Is Analogous to the Political

The politics, the political ideas, the political philosophy of Kant can be unpacked only if one already knows what is political and what is not, and what is Kant's and what is not. On the basis of certain texts signed by Kant, and with a perspective, an *Absicht*, which is not necessarily Kant's own but which can pride itself on its being according to Kant (as in the way Kant often writes, *der Idee nach* [*selon l'Idée*], according to the Idea)—these texts being considered political by some and not by others—one can try to determine what has been given to be phrased by the opening declaration of this Center, namely, the political [*le politique*] (which is not politics [*la politique*]) in its "retreat." It could just as well be said that the "choice" of this perspective, which leads us to give preference to certain texts in the Kantian corpus, is itself the result of a "political decision."

If I could justify this decision, it would mean that I already knew what it would be to legitimate a decision, that is, a judgment, and that I already knew, at least in good part, what the political is, and even much more than the political. But I can at least try to explain how it is that Kant's texts on law, essentially the *Doctrine of Right*, and more particularly his doctrine of public right—which it may appear impertinent or unjust to leave out of the Kantian political corpus—turn out here to be if not ignored, then at least disregarded. This question regarding the corpus brings us to the heart of the subject, a subject that was debated during the discussion after [Jean-Luc—Trans.] Nancy's talk, when he was reproached for not restricting himself to an internal critique of the Hegelian text.[1]

The philosophical phrase according to Kant is an analog of the political phrase according to Kant. But it can only be analogous to the extent that it is critical and not doctrinal. The doctrinal, or systematic, phrase ought to come after the critical phrase; its rules are in the regulation indicated by the idea of system, it is an organ of the organic body of phrases that is doctrine; it is a legitimated phrase.[2] To be established as such, its claim to validity had to be judged; if it claims to speak the true, to be judged whether and how it achieves this; if it claims to speak the just or the good, to be judged whether and how it achieves this, and so on. These judgments bearing on the respective claims of various phrase families (cognitive, ethical, juridical, and so forth), and these verdicts establishing the respective validity of each of these within its field, its territory or domain,[3] are the work of critique. It's known that Kant often symbolizes the activity of critique as being like that of a court of justice or a judge.[4] Nonetheless, this judge cannot be a magistrate, does not dispose of any judiciary, criminal, or civil code, not even a casebook, to lead an inquiry or formulate a verdict. This judge does not judge claims according to the measure of an established and irrefutable law. That law must in turn fall under the purview of the judge's examination. From this point of view, critical philosophy is in the condition of an instance that must declare "this is the case, this phrase is the right one" (with regard to the true, the beautiful, the good, even the just), rather than that of an instance—utterly illusory, moreover, in Kant's eyes first of all—which need only apply, without any other form of procedure, an already established rule of evaluation to a new datum. This is not to say that this instance has no other evaluative criterion at its disposal but that the applicability of the criterion to the case is itself subject to evaluation. Then, either an infinitely regressive research into criteria of criteria must be admitted, which de facto prohibits judgment, or else it will be necessary to rely on that "gift of nature," which is judgment and which allows us to say: here, this is the case. For, according to Kant, it is the case of philosophy, as critique, to say: this is the case.

In the Architectonic section of the *Critique of Pure Reason*, Kant defines a "school concept [scholarly, *Schulbegriff*] of philosophy." According to this concept, the goal of philosophy is to construct the systematic unity of knowledge, that is, to attain "the *logical* perfection of knowledge." He opposes this to a "world concept" (worldly or cosmic, *Weltbegriff*), according to which "philosophy is the science of the relation of all knowledge to the essential ends of human reason." According to the *Schulbegriff,* the philosopher is an "artist of reason [*ein Vernunftkünstler*]"; according to the *Weltbegriff,* he is the "legislator of human reason [*der Gesetzgeber der menschlichen Vernunft*]."[5] This philosopher is a "prototype," individualized in "the ideal of the *philosopher,*" meaning in the ideal philosopher. He is "the master" of the mathematician, the natural philosopher, and the logician, making use of them as "instruments" in order to "advance the essential ends of human reason." We are tempted to look for names to attach to this ideal, but Kant adds, "Him alone [this master] we must call *the philosopher*; but he himself is found nowhere, while the idea of his legislation is encountered everywhere in every human reason" (*KRV* 694–95).

The philosophical ideal is thus not to build systems but to judge the claims to validity of all "knowledges" (which I call phrases), and this in their respective relations with the essential ends of human reason. For this evaluation, the critic has eyes, or at least *one* eye, which is directed toward a type, which is an ideal: the philosopher. The ideal is not the Idea: the latter "gives the rule, [the former] serves as the prototype for the complete determination of the copy" (*KRV* 486). The ideal allows us to measure the gap between the theoretical or practical result attained by the critical enquiry and the perfection of the judgment. It thus allows us to say more justifiably of a phrase claiming to be true or just, and so on: this is the case. The ideal is a mode of the presentation (the *Darstellung*) of an object able to serve as an intuition for a concept of reason, which by definition cannot have one, that is, an Idea. It allows for a complete determination of a good copy, while resting on an indeterminacy, since it is the projection into one order—here, the order of Ideas—of a presentation that is pertinent to another—here, the presentation of an individual, the philosopher.

This ideal allows the philosopher to determine more completely the gap between his actual critical thought and philosophical thought that is absolute, that is, legislative of human reason. Which means: establishing the rules of formation and validation for all possible phrases. And it is under the cover of this ideal, of the presentation of what is not immediately presentable, that philosophy goes out beyond the school and becomes what it must be, philosophy in the world. What is at stake for philosophy is to be, not a technology of systems, but a legislation of the powers to know. The perfect and sufficiently determinable legislator that the philosopher must be is, however, never directly presentable in the form of an example, that is, of an intuition directly presenting the object of an empirical concept (*KUK* 225). The philosopher is not localizable *in concreto* (*KRV* 694), but just like the ideal of practical reason, which is the wise man according to the Stoics, the philosopher is locatable *in individuo*, "as a singular thing, determinable or wholly determined by the Idea alone" (*KRV* 551). For this individual is nowhere, while the Idea for which he is a kind of schema within the order that is his own "is encountered everywhere in every human reason," as we have already read. Guided by the ideal of the philosopher, the critical philosopher can then say of a phrase that claims to be philosophical that such is indeed the case. But his judgment is not a determining one because he is guided only by a rule of indirect presentation of the object of the Idea, and not by a rule of direct presentation, like a schema.

Nonetheless, it is by judging for every phrase whether it is the case, guided in a nondetermined fashion by the ideal of the philosopher, that the philosopher goes out beyond the schoolyard and enters the world, and that philosophy is not only theoretically correct, but that it is also able to be of practical value. However, the world is itself the object of an Idea.[6] Nor does it give rise to a direct presentation, only to an indirect one. There are several possible indirect modes of presentation. The one that concerns the ideal of the philosopher is the one by which the world is presented as a nature.[7] For it is as nature that the world is judged to be commensurable with "the essential ends of human reason," which are what regulate the ideal evaluation of the philosopher as legislator. So much so that in his critical activity, the philosopher is not only guided, though in a not immediately determined fashion, by the ideal of the philosopher, but he is also guided by the Idea of a nature that does not refuse to present, be it indirectly, objects to judgment of which it can be said that it is the case (physical nature, but also nature in man). Of this nature, it must be said as of the ideal of the philosopher that it is nowhere, that it is to say, that it is not presentable by intuition; it must also be said, as of the Idea of the philosopher, that it is present "everywhere in every human reason."

We can thus make the following argument: that to philosophize in terms of critique is not only to describe the rules that govern the formation of different phrase families but also to present objects for each that allow us to judge that "this is the case"; that what has just been enunciated is itself a judgment that asserts that such is the case for the critical phrase; that the presentable case when the critical phrase is involved is not an object that can be intuited but the object of an Idea (of philosophy) whose mode of presentation remains to be determined; and finally, that, whatever this mode may be, it presupposes in any case (thus again under the rubric of the object of an Idea) that every phrase can find on the side of objects, an object that can be presented to it in such a way as to validate it, hence that the set of objects is, in ways that remain to be specified, in affinity with the requirement of presentation entailed by critique. This affinity of the entirety of objects to the possibility of judgment is what makes of this entirety a nature.

This is the condition of a philosophy that thinks by *Weltbegriff.* If we do not accept this condition, then we remain enclosed within the schoolyard; we perfect the logic of systems, but we do not concern ourselves with the "essential ends of human reason"; and we can peaceably indulge in the affliction that threatens every thinker, the one which results from the suspicion that thought is incommensurable with its objects: the "thoroughly displeasing representation" that comes from a "heterogeneity" between the world of objects and thought, such that no phrase "beyond the most common experience" would be able to validate itself in any presentation (*KUK* 74). In the Kantian political phrase, we will in good stead come again across this argument—*but* is it an argument?— by threat of disgust. It is a matter of the interests of reason.

If, however, we do not allow ourselves to be intimidated by this threat, we could ask Kant: How does the critical philosopher judge then that it is the case when there is no intuition to present for the case?

In the *Critique of Judgment*, Kant distinguishes between two modes of presentation or hypotyposis. For determinant judgments, that is, when it is a matter of descriptive phrases, either they are based on experience (empirical concepts), and intuition presents objects to them in the mode of *examples*; or else they are based in knowledge (pure a priori concepts), and pure intuition presents objects to them in the mode of *schemata*. When it is a matter of ideas, where by definition intuition cannot present anything in the way of an object, presentation takes place indirectly through analogy: "An intuition is submitted such that in relation to it the procedure of the faculty of judgment is merely analogous to what it observes in the course of schematizing" (*KUK* 197). The form of presentation, which is that of the intuitive mode (schemata), is disengaged from the intuitable content, since it is absent, and under this form is placed another intuition, "also empirical," which in sum allows the Idea to be validated as if it were a concept of the understanding. In other words, the noncognitive (descriptive, but dialectical) phrase is presented with an "as if" referent, a referent that would be its own were the phrase a cognitive one. This indirect presentation is called symbolical, or presentation through *symbols*.

In this way the critical philosopher can continue to judge a phrase, even when there is no empirical case directly presentable to validate it. This mode of presentation saves him from dipping into the technology of systems or corpus of doctrine, and from restricting himself miserably to an internal critique. By analogy, every properly philosophical—that is, critical—phrase operates as an external critique, and *must* do so, if it seeks in any way to conform to its Idea. Because it consists in judging, and more particularly in finding *analoga* (symbols or others) for presenting its Ideas (including the idea of itself), philosophy cannot be learned: "We can at best only learn *to philosophize*" (*KRV* 694). By contrast, doctrine, and in particular the doctrine of right, can be learned, it does not really need judgment, since on the contrary it presupposes its prior use in the critical phrase. That is at least what is in principle implied by Kant in the very title of the *Doctrine of Right*.

It remains, on this first point, for the assertion to be argued that this reflective condition—the one that condemns the presentation of phrase objects to the operation of analogy and of which we've just established that it is the condition of critique according to Kant—is analogous to the condition of the political according to Kant. This argumentation constitutes the basis of this study. I will settle for the moment with recalling a text that bears witness to the spontaneous self-evidence of this analogy.

Having to introduce the *Critique of Pure Reason*, Kant in the preface to the first edition of the book, paints a portrait of its context and tells the tale of its genealogy. In the beginning, he writes, dogmatism ruled despotically over metaphysics; the legislation of this *despotism* "bore traces of ancient barbarism." Later, "through intestine wars" this despotism gave way to a "complete *anarchy*," and "the *skeptics*, a kind of nomad, despising all settled modes of life, broke up from time to time the social bond [*die bürgerliche Vereinigung*]." Thereafter, in modern times, it was believed that with Locke's "*physiology* of the human understanding," the "legitimation" of the respective claims was acquired. In reality, this was nothing more than a renewal of dogmatism. "Today," pursues Kant, "after all paths (as we believe) have been used in vain, there reigns distaste [*Ueberdruss*, surfeit, *taedium*] and complete *indifferentism*." This attitude "engenders chaos and darkness in the sciences," but it is at the same time "the source, or at least the prelude [*das Vorspiel*] of an impending transformation and *Aufklärung* of those same sciences, which an ill-applied zeal has rendered obscure, confused, and unusable." Kant then underscores, in passing, that the indifferentist attitude is impossible when it is a question of enquiries "to whose object human nature *cannot* be *indifferent*." Then, with apparent inconsequence, he observes that indifference, *Gleichgültikeit*, is "a phenomenon [*Phänomen*] deserving attention and reflection [*Nachsinnen*]. This is evidently not the effect of levity [*des Leichtsinns*], but of a *faculty of judgment* come to maturity in an age that refuses any longer to be lulled by the mere appearance of knowledge; it is a call to reason to undertake anew the most difficult of all its tasks, namely, that of self-knowledge [*Selbstverständnis*], and to institute a tribunal [*ein Gerichtshof*] that will secure [*sichere*] reason's legitimate claims." And Kant concludes, "This tribunal is none other than the *critique of pure reason*" (*KRV* 100–101).

A political context, and genealogy following a two-step repetitive, compulsive rhythm. Metaphysics is a *Kampfplatz* [battlefield] (*KRV* 99), an arena where claims to legitimacy confront each other. Between the despot and the nomad, writes Kant, "I have set forth on this path, the only one left." This course in metaphysical things, leading up to the *Gleichgültigkeit*, prepares the time of Critique. The tribunal is called to order to examine the requests of two opposing parties, the same ones that are judged in the Antithetic, but that is possible only because thought has first gone through the disabused impartiality of "it's all the same." The state of indifference liberates and ripens the power to decide between [*la puissance de départager*], that is, the strength to judge, which, for thought, is the strength to judge itself.

The story that presents the instituting of the critical tribunal is a narration, perhaps nothing more than a "novel." How should we take it? In critical terms, that is to say, from the point of view of the judge himself, Kant by this story pleads the cause of criticism before the tribunal, over and against the two plaintiffs, dogmatism and skepticism. His plea contains a *narratio*, which must be examined critically, under the regimen of the question: What case is this? A phrase of experience (historiography)? Or cognition (history in the sense of *Historie*)? Or dialectics (the Idea of reason)? Or poetics (the Idea of imagination)? In any case, the narrative's end is determined by its effect, which is the institution of the tribunal itself. It supposes a teleology in the course of metaphysical conflicts. It is by resorting to this teleology that narrative flaunts its claim to legitimate the tribunal of critique. But the judge is not in need of legitimation in order to judge, the faculty that states "this is the case" could not accept a genealogy that would be exempt in principle from its examination. It's in Hegel that the story of the engenderment of *Weltgericht* from *Weltgeschichte* is at one and the same time a judgment handed down by the tribunal.

If the judge does not need the story, why then does Kant have recourse to it? We need to turn the question around: Why would he forbid it? It's a concatenation of phrases that is sensible, that can be argued, and for certain of its phrases objects of experience can be presented. Where it is certain that no intuition can be presented as an object permitting the phrase to be evaluated, this applies to the entire narrative, for as has been said, this entirety is only given relative to an Idea of end, namely, the institution of the critical tribunal, which by concept would be, retroactively, the cause of the sequence of metaphysical combats. In sum, it is necessary to judge how the event of the critique is presentable. It is certainly presentable according to several phrase families, and the judge must examine each of these according to the criterion of presentation that is pertinent to it. The story as totality will appear elsewhere, as a kind of "sweet" narration, meaning one that gives pleasure and provides hope of a final meaning where it seemed absent, on the battlefield of doctrines. Other presentations of the institution of the tribunal must also be possible. The judge does not exclude them in advance; he welcomes them, examines them, and determines the rules for their respective validity. In a word, he recognizes the heterogeneity of phrase families vis-à-vis each other; he disentangles them: he decides, but he admits, subject to further examination, their coexistence: he compromises. The *Kampfplatz* stays open, but the judge replaces the doctrines with their uncritiqued claims by phrase families whose respective rules are established by the "this is the case" that limits their validity. And henceforth, it is between phrase families that the battle will take place, this time on a critical battlefield. (And in my narrative of the history of philosophy, this is where the Wittgenstein of the *Philosophical Investigations* directly picks up the relay of criticism. That is why I use the expression *phrase family* where Kant says *representation*.)

Finally, if we ask whence the judge holds his authority, the answer is that he does not hold it, that his authority awaits him, since the phrase of judgment, the phrase that says "this is the case," which is critical philosophizing, itself presupposes, as we have seen, the family of Ideas, that of philosophy and that of nature. This family has a right only to indirect presentations, without schemata or even examples, but only with symbols.

By this commentary on the text of the preface, I hope to have criticized what appeared to go "without saying" in the analogy of the critical with the political. And at the same time, I hope to have explained why the *Doctrine of Right* does not appear to me to be a pertinent text for the study of the political in Kant.

2

The Archipelago

Kant's historico-political texts are dispersed, generally speaking, among the three *Critiques* and a dozen minor works. The Critique of Political Reason was never written. Within certain limits to be determined, it is legitimate to see in this dispersion, whatever its "cause," (which the phrase of understanding, the cognitive phrase dumbly demands), a sign (we will come back to this word) of a particular heterogeneity of the political as "object" of phrases. This heterogeneity of the object is already noticeable in the third *Critique*. The faculty of judging is supplied not with a proper object of its own, but with at least two: art and nature. I say "at least" because it is a question, the whole question perhaps, of knowing whether this faculty of judgment is a faculty. Kant previously gave this word a precise meaning, that of a potential of phrases subordinate to a group of rules for their formation and presentation (in the Kantian sense), when it was a question of sensibility, of the understanding, and of reason for what is theoretical, and of reason for what is practical. But in fact, judgment intervenes already and necessarily every time it is a question of saying that "this is the case" to validate a phrase, hence for presenting an object allowing this validation, which takes place among cognitives under the regimen of the schemata, among dialectical argumentatives under that of the symbol, among prescriptives, when evaluating responsibility and morality, under the regimen of types.

In the introduction to the third *Critique*, the dispersion of phrase families is not merely recognized, it is dramatized to the point that the problem raised is that of finding "passages" (*Uebergänge*) between these kinds of heterogeneous phrases. And the "faculty" of judgment, by reason of its very ubiquity, as I've just recalled, that is to say, on account of its being called upon every time a phrase needs to be validated by a presentation, appears in this text as a power of "passages" between the faculties, to the point that the faculty of judgment is recognized as having a major privilege in the matter of its unifying capacity and at the same time a major flaw in the matter of its capacity to cognize an object that is its own, to wit: that it has no determined object. That is why we may wonder whether it is indeed a faculty of knowledge in the Kantian sense. Among all the families of phrases, no matter how heterogeneous they may be relative to each other, what Kant stubbornly maintains (though perhaps it is his problematics of the subject that stubbornly maintains itself in its place) in calling the faculty of judgment is the determination of the mode of presentation of the object that respectively suits each of these families.

If in turn an object must be presented for the Idea of the faculties' shifting gears if we understand them as capacities for knowledge in a large sense, that is, as capacities to have objects (sometimes as domains, sometimes as territories, sometimes as fields) (*KUK* 10), and since the object suitable to be presented for validating the dispersion of the faculties must necessarily be a symbol, I would propose an archipelago. Each phrase family would be like an island; the faculty of judgment would be, at least in part, like an outfitter or an admiral who launches expeditions from one island to another sent out to present to the one what they have found (invented, in the old sense of the word) in the other, and which might serve to the first one as an "as-if" intuition to validate it. This force of intervention, be it war or commerce, has no object; it has no island, but it requires a milieu, namely the sea, the *Archipelagos*, the principal sea as the Aegean was once called. This sea bears another name in the introduction to the third *Critique*, that of field, *Feld*: "Concepts, insofar as they are related to objects, regardless of whether a cognition of the latter is possible or not, have their field, which is determined merely in accordance with the relation that their object has to our faculty of cognition in general" (*KUK* 61). The end of this same introduction teaches us that this faculty of cognition *in general* includes the understanding, the faculty of judging, and reason. It would be at least just and moreover in conformity with what is indicated in the "stepladder" of representations Kant puts together at the end of the section on "Ideas in General" in the Dialectic of the first *Critique* (*KRV* 398), if we added sensibility. All these faculties find their object in the field, some carve out a territory, others a domain, but the faculty of judging finds neither one nor the other; it assures the passages between those of the others. It is more of a faculty of the milieu, within which all of the circumscriptions of legitimacy are captured. Moreover, that faculty is also what has permitted the delimiting of territories and domains and what has established the authority of each family over its island. And it has only been able to do this thanks to the commerce or warfare it fosters between them.

There's a means here to situate some passages. I'll indicate a few without claiming to exhaust their enumeration or analyze their singular regimens. The transcendental illusion, for instance. How do we know that dialectical phrases that have the form of cognitive phrases are not cognitive? And that, in so doing, the territory of the reasoning's validity does not coincide with the domain of the understanding's legislation? This is because we cannot present an intuitable object for argumentative phrases, that is to say, an object given in space and time. Reason is urged on by its need (*Bedürfnis*) (*KRV* 396) to maximize the concept; it obeys a "solely logical prescription [*eine bloss logische Vorschrift*]" (*KRV* 392) to move toward what is unconditioned. What is presentable to the phrase of reason as an object able to legitimate it cannot be a phenomenon. The critique here consists, once the formation rule for the phrase (to reason is to conclude by means of the universal) has been identified, in playing the rule of presentation, after which the dialectical phrase is "isolated" (insulated) from the phrase of understanding. The transcendental illusion does not on that account disappear, but it is exposed (*KRV* 386). The *as if* that is the source of this illusion is righted: the dialectical phrase acts as if it were speaking of phenomena, the critique requires that it speaks of "as-if" phenomena. Of symbols, that is, among which we find the one we have already encountered under the name of the ideal.

Another eminent case of a "passage" in operation is indicated in § 59 of the third *Critique*, where it is a matter of showing that "the beautiful is the symbol of the morally good" (*KUK* 227). And from there, the analysis of the symbolizing operation, to which allusion has previously been made. This is a double operation and is called analogy. It consists in "first applying the concept to the object of a sensible intu- ition, and then, second, applying the mere rule of the reflection on that intuition to a completely different object, of which the first is only the symbol" (*KUK* 226). Kant gives two examples (but are these examples in the sense previously stated? Can there be an intuitional presentation of symbols, which are indirect presentations? This would need to be exam- ined as a case of a "passage" made over a "passage"), and so Kant gives two examples of symbols: a mere machine, a hand mill, may symbolize a monarchical state "ruled by a single absolute will"; an organic body may symbolize a monarchical state "ruled in accordance with laws internal to the people." In both cases, there is no resemblance between the symbol- ized object and the symbolizing one, which is "completely different." But there is an identity established between the rule of reflection applied to the second example and the one applied to the first.

So it goes, according to Kant, for the passage between the beautiful and the good. The rule of reflection made on these two objects presents the same characteristics—immediacy, disinterestedness, freedom, uni- versality—but its application differs in each case. Immediacy is applied to the sensible in the case of the beautiful, to the concept in the case of the good. In the judgment of taste, freedom is that of the imagination coming into agreement with the concept; in moral judgment, it is that of the will coming into agreement with itself, and so on. The analogy at work here is certainly not identical with the one that presents a hand mill or an organic body as symbols of political regimes. It is so lacking in identity that, rigorously speaking, it is impossible to consider the ob- ject of taste as a phenomenon on the same level as the hand mill or the organic body. These can be given through a *Versinnlichung*, an operation of sensibility in accordance with the laws of the understanding alone (at least as concerns the hand mill), but Kant is the first to emphasize that *Sinnlichkeit* and the understanding are not sufficient to grasp (and thus to constitute) the object of taste. With the question of the beautiful, it "is the *intelligible* toward which taste looks," he writes; "the faculty of judgment does not see itself as subjected to a heteronomy of the laws of experience"; it "sees itself related to something . . . which is neither nature nor freedom, . . . the supersensible" (*KUK* 227). And if there is "sensation" in the experience of the beautiful, it is in a completely different sense than sensation as established in the Transcendental Aesthetic of the first *Critique*: "If a determination of the feeling of pleasure or pain is called sensation, this expression signifies something entirely different than if I call the representation of a thing (through sense, as a receptivity belonging to the faculty of cognition) sensation" (*KUK* 92).

If a symbol of the good takes place through the beautiful, it is not therefore because the latter is a phenomenon that can be intuited directly and that comes in the place of some other object, the good, for which we have no intuition. The analogy here works instead in reverse, namely on the fact that the beautiful *is not* an experiential object in the sense that there is no sensible presentation *either*, but that it is determined by a certain concatenation of the faculties (in accordance with the four operators cited earlier) and that this concatenation reoccurs, according to the same operations but differently applied, when the mind is turned toward the good. It is therefore, a "symbolics," not through a substitution of objects but through the transferal and rotation of an intra-faculty mechanism: a group of rules for forming phrases (the four operators isolated by Kant) is transferred, after being altered, from the pull of the feeling of pleasure and pain to that of the faculty of desiring, without us ever being able to speak of a direct presentation. Here again, there is certainly "commerce" and "passage" from one island to the next, and, if you like "presentation" within the ethics of something that belongs to taste, but that something is not an intuitable object. The acceptation one needs to give to the term *presentation* is thereby widened to the extent that the expeditions made by the faculty of judging to adjacent islands do not just bring back intuitable objects but even rules for phrases that are solely "logical" or formal. Conclusive bits of evidence, those that allow one to say "this is the case," get complicated.

The same goes for another no less eminent "passage," which Kant calls *type* in the section "Of the Typic of Pure Practical Judgment," in the second chapter of the Analytic of Pure Practical Reason.[1] It is stated there that the maxim of action must "stand the test as to the form of a law of nature in general, or else it is morally impossible." Why? "This is how," writes Kant, "even the most common understanding judges; for the law of nature always lies at the basis of its most ordinary judgments, even those of experience." Whenever a deed that is either done or to be done needs evaluation, the understanding, which, Kant continues, "has the law of nature always at hand," makes "that *law of nature* merely the type of a *law of freedom*." It does not carry intuitions over into the ethical domain, but only "the form of *Gesetzmässigkeit* [of 'what is within the scope of the law,' let's say: of legalization] in general." This "passage" is thus a common one, but why is there a need to cast a paradoxical bridgehead of nature into the domain of freedom? A type is needed because without it, writes Kant, the law of pure practical reason could not provide "use in application" (*KPV* 196). When the law is theoretical, the schema is what is charged with the application of intuitive data and what guides the judgment in determining that "such is indeed the case." But in the practical domain, the Idea of the Good is what the judgment needs to regulate itself, and there is no scheme for the Idea. "But no intuition can be put under the law of freedom (as that of a causality not sensibly conditioned)—and hence under the concept of the unconditioned good as well—and hence no schema on behalf of its application *in concreto*" (*KPV* 196).

What makes the passage is thus not the form of the intuition or schema, but the form of the law, or rather of the *Gesetzmässigkeit*. Ethical judgment borrows this form from the theoretical in order to guide itself in establishing the case: "Ask yourself whether, if the action you propose were to take place by a law of the nature of which you were yourself a part, you could indeed regard it as possible through your will" (*KPV* 196). The *type* of legislation is what formally guides the maxim of the will in the formulation of the categorical imperative, as well as in the evaluation of just action. The *so dass* of the *Handelt so dass* of the categorical imperative must therefore be understood as an *as if* [comme si] rather than a *so that* [de sorte que]: for universality cannot be effectively concluded from the maxim but only presented indirectly to the evaluation that is made of it.

This "type" is also what explains why an Idea that does not make obvious sense is introduced into the problematics of ethics, namely the Idea of a supersensible nature. If there were not the "as if it were a mechanical nature," to transfer legalization from the domain of cognition into the moral domain, the Idea of "all practical rational beings" would have no pertinence in that domain, and at the same time, by a supplementary "passage," the idea of a cosmopolitan society would have no pertinence in the historico-political domain. It is because there is such a type of legislation that supersensible nature not only is the object of a possible Idea, but that it can be presented as archetypal (*urbildliche*) for an ectypal (*nachgebildete*) nature that is a copy (*Gegenbild*) of the former in the sensory world (*KPV* 175). The thematics of type ("typographics," as Philippe Lacoue-Labarthe would say[2]) surely comes down from Plato, but here it is recast within a completely different problematics, not so much on account of its being post-Cartesian and centered on the subject, but rather because it is not so, inasmuch as it loosens the links between the faculties of knowledge to the point that these links are often no more than "passages," adventurous transfers of devices or forms, borrowings that are necessarily paradoxical since they are not pertinent to the domain in which they are applied, at the same time that they are nonetheless indispensable to their circumscription.

It is not possible here to draw up the inventory of "passages." There are less notorious ones, though no less strange. Let me cite for the record that "passage" Kant ventures to present in the first *Critique* as an "Ideal of sensibility" and that he calls "*monogram*" (*KRV* 552). It is, he writes, "a wavering sketch drawn from diverse experiences," an "incommunicable phantom" in the judgment of painters (and physiognomists), an "inimitable model for possible empirical intuitions," which do not "provide any rule capable of being defined and examined." Kant turns this shadowy something into a creation of the imagination. But this imaginary is not an Idea of the imagination; it is an ideal, and an ideal of sensibility, because it is a kind of schema, an "as-if" schema, of the Idea of the imagination within the domain (or field?) of sensory experience. Here again it is not a rule, but an "as-if" rule, a regulatory conveyance from the imagination into sensibility. And beyond that, and more basically, there is the Idea of the imagination itself, which is only constituted by a reverse passage from reason to the imagination: a conceptless intuition in the place of an intuitionless concept. As for this "passage," there is no need to underscore its importance for communicating between subjective and objective teleology.

I could go on; we'll find other passages in the historico-political field. A final observation, though, with regard to the archipelago: in the "Concluding Remark on the Resolution of the Mathematical-Transcendental Ideas, and Preamble to the Resolution of the Dynamical-Transcendental Ideas" (*KRV* 530ff.), Kant makes it clear that when it is an issue of settling the antinomies among the former, the judge is obligated to dismiss both parties, since the only objects they could present that would legitimate their respective thesis and antithesis statements would be "conditions *within phenomena*"; "in the two mathematical-transcendental antinomies, we had no *object* other than that which is within phenomena" (*KRV* 531). Now, neither party can present such an object, since their phrases are Idea phrases, and not concepts of the understanding. But with the dynamical antinomies (those of freedom and of the supreme being), "an entirely new prospect" is opened up. There, "the suit in which reason is implicated, which had previously been *dismissed*, . . . may be settled—since the judge may supply what is lacking [*ergänst den Mangel*] in the legal principles [*Rechtsgründe*] that were misrecognized on both sides [in the first two antinomies]—by an *arrangement* [a transaction, *vergleichen*] to the satisfaction [*Genugtuung*] of both parties" (*KRV*).

All of this is nothing more than an exposition of the conditions for the synthesis of heterogeneity. But it is done in such a manner that it is clear that this synthesis is not *de jure*, and that the judge compromises [*transige*] here without there being a rule that authorizes him to do so, unless it be the principle that heterogeneity ought to be affirmatively respected. This will be the case for resolving the antinomy of practical reason, for resolving the antinomy of taste, and eminently so, for resolving the antinomy of the faculty of judgment in § 69–71 of the third *Critique*. Eminently so, for it is stated there, in the prolongation of what is "lacking in the legal principles" from the Antinomy of the first *Critique*, that "the faculty of judgment must serve as its own principle" (*KUK* 258), and it is stated there in the prolongation of the "arrangement" found between the two parties in the first *Critique*, that a similar arrangement is possible between the purposive thesis and the mechanistic antithesis, between the thesis of nature and that of the world, since the former, which is that of the faculty of the, properly reflective, judgment, which is "autonomous" (*KUK* 261), takes nothing from the "heteronomous" usage (*KUK*) of the determinant faculty, which takes the opposite side. The name born by this transaction is that of "guiding thread [*fil conducteur, Leitfaden*]."[3] The guiding thread is the way in which the reflective judgment, attentive to singularities left aside by the cognitive phrase, "seeking" them out to find an order there (*KUK* 258), freely presupposes this order, that is to say, judges it as if there were an order there. If the thread is one that guides, it is because it has an end. But this end cannot be directly presented as an object: "that causality [by an end] is a mere Idea, to which one by no means undertakes to concede reality" (*KUK* 260–61).

Once more, then, the judge settles the legitimacy of claims to validity. In so doing, he slices the transcendental subject into insular faculties, and he trenches the field of all possible objects into an archipelago. But he also seeks out "passages" that attest to the coexistence of heterogeneous families, and which allow transactions that are to the satisfaction of various parties. If the judge appears "transigent," it is because the judge is nothing other than the faculty of judgment, critique, and that critique can trenchantly decide only on the condition that it ought to be able to intervene in all the islands of the archipelago, only on the condition that, it at least, can "pass" without any rule, "before" rules, whether analogically or otherwise, in order to establish them.

3

What Is Delivered in Enthusiasm

The importance of the philosophy of the beautiful and the sublime in the first part of the third *Critique* resides in the de-realizing of the object of aesthetic feelings, and at the same time, in the absence of a faculty of aesthetic cognition, properly speaking. The same goes, in perhaps an even more radical fashion, for the historico-political object, which has no reality in and of itself, and for a faculty of political cognition, which must remain nonexistent. What does have a reality, that is, what has a concept for which intuitions can be presented, is solely the phenomena, all of them conditioned and conditioning, whose series (which is itself never given) constitutes the, not even natural, but solely cosmological history of humanity. The series is never given, it becomes the object of an Idea, and, by dint of the human world, falls under the same antithetics as the cosmological series in general. Certainly, as in the case of experience, the phrase of understanding, that is, scientific cognition, is always possible for the sequences of the series for which there can be intuitional presentations. But, by definition, these sequences of conditioning and conditioned phenomena must have regularity, and hence be repeated, be it in the form of progress, regression, or eternal return through stagnation.[1] The phrase signifying repetition in the series, whether the latter be the object of an ascending or descending synthesis, is thus legitimate on the condition that objects corresponding to it are presented within phenomena: "The human being is an *animal* which . . . *has need of a master.* . . . But then this master is exactly as much an animal who has need of a master."[2] "Man hates slavery, but a new slavery is needed to get rid of the old."[3] Or again, to refute the hope of progress through education: "Since they are also *human beings* who must effect this education, consequently such beings who themselves have to be educated for that purpose" (*Conflict* 308). These regularities are not laws that are merely empirical; they can be established via statistical tables (*Idea* 108) that make evident the a priori character of the categories that serve to synthesize the data into series, the categories of (mechanical) causality and of reciprocal action.

The cognitive phrase, with its twin criteria of pertinence with regard to negation (the principle of contradiction) and pertinence with regard to intuitional presentation, is in Kant generally in opposition to vain hopes, false promises, and prophecies. The cognitive phrase is what is used to refute the right to insurrection and to condemn the violent substitution of one authority for another. The argument goes as follows: the existence of the common being (*das gemeine Wesen*) is the referent for a phrase that is cognitive (of the understanding) or at best teleologically objective (finality within organized beings). This common being's proximity to the good is judged in a teleologically subjective phrase (moral finality within reasonable beings). Revolution breaks (*Abbruch*) an existing common being; another one cannot fail to replace it (natural law). The heterogeneity of the two phrase families is not modified. Revolutionary politics is based on a transcendental illusion in the political domain: it confuses what can be presented as an object for a cognitive phrase with what can be presented as an object for a speculative and/or ethical phrase; that is to say, it confuses schemata or examples with *analoga*. The progress toward betterment of a common being is not judged by empirical intuitions but by signs.[4]

In the case of the descending series, on top of the difficulty encountered by the synthesis of the ascending series (which stems from the fact that its totality and its beginning are not able to be intuited) there is the difficulty of linking on effects which are not yet there, and for which one cannot present documents, as one can for causes. Even worse: it can be admitted that the synthesis of descending series (that is, of phenomena yet to come) does not even require a speculative, transcendental Idea. The antinomy of the indefinite raises the problem of the beginning of cosmological series, but not of their end. Kant writes in the first *Critique*, "If we make ourselves an idea . . . of the whole series of all *future* alterations in the world, then it is just a being of reason [*ens rationis*], which is thought up only arbitrarily, and not presupposed necessarily by reason" (*KRV* 407). I will not here discuss, important as it is, the relation between an Idea (a concept without intuition) and a being of reason, which is an empty, objectless concept, such as examined on the last page of the Analytic of the first *Critique* (382–83). Speculatively speaking, there is ahead of us, in cosmological time at least, *nothing*, neither as object, nor even as determined concept.

To these limitations on the claims of the theoretical phrase regarding the human cosmological series, is added a final one, which Kant underscores with some solemnity in the article, *On the Use of Teleological Principles in Philosophy*,[5] with regard to nature. It is necessary, he writes, to distinguish the description of nature from its history, physiography from physiogony. These two domains "are entirely *heterogeneous*," the description of nature is displayed with all the splendor of a grand system, the history of nature "can only exhibit fragments or shaky hypotheses," a "silhouette" of science, where "for most questions a blank [*Vacat*] might well remain." (There follows a long apology of Kant by Kant against Forster on the theme: I have exerted scrupulous care to keep the sciences from encroaching on each other's limits.) What this is really all about is the regressive synthesis, moving toward the beginnings of the history of the world. If blanks must remain there, it can readily be understood why: intuitions would need to be able to be presented to the physiogonic phrase for all of the singular existences inscribed in the series. Here, even an example is not sufficient, and schemata even less so. The presentational requirement presses on sensation most closely, documentation is needed for everything, and yet the series is no more than an Idea! The same would go for an anthropogony.

There it is, in sum, for the cognitive phrase: it does not have much to say about history that could be validated by the critical judge. In fact, it remains unaware of the historico-*political* because it stays under the rule of intuitional presentation. There are still many other possible phrase families. Their presentational rules are different. One might expect to see analogy at work there, or more generally, "passage." It would not be possible here to conduct a complete survey of the terms that mark the interfaculty sharing of the historico-political field and that indicate on the object side a contradictory determination, or so to speak, an indeterminate determination. From this Kantian lexicology of the historico-political, I have retained only two terms of unequal importance, one that occurs frequently in the *Idea* of 1784, the other in the *Conflict with the Faculty of Law* of 1797. The first is the term *guiding thread* (*Leitfaden*), the other being the *sign of history* (*Geschichtszeichen*). They both serve to phrase the historico-political, but they are not of the same order; the first is a symbol, the second the properly critical denomination of an important interfaculty point of passage.

The *Idea for a Universal History from a Cosmopolitan Point of View* (1784) makes the following argument about the nature of discourse concerning the historico-political: if one clings to immediate intuitive data, political history is chaos. It arouses an *Unwillen* (an indignant spite, depression) because it suggests that this lamentable spectacle proceeds from "a purposelessly playing nature [*zwecklos spielende*]," where "desolate chance [*das trostlose Ungefähr*] takes the place of the guiding thread of reason" (*Idea* 109). Now, it is not just, in the critical sense, to stick to the moroseness of dismal happenstance, that is to say, to the certification of non-sense. Why? The affect that accompanies this description is itself a sign: if there is a feeling of pain with regard to the phrasing of the historico-political field in terms of the absurd, that is the negative index that another ability to phrase, by Ideas, another possible genre of discourse, one for which the Idea of freedom is at stake, cannot link onto that world on account of its absurdity. For it is at least in the practical interests of reason that this ability not see itself forbidden from the historical-political phrase. From this point of view, it is observed that there in effect exists within the human species natural dispositions, which are in affinity (*abgezielt*) with the use of reason, as testified by the very existence of philosophy (*Idea*); if human history were but sound and fury, it would have to be admitted then that nature, though it has endowed humankind with its dispositions and deposited these "germs" of the development of reason in human beings, would have moreover deprived humanity of the necessary means to use that reason (*Idea* 25). The supreme absurdity: "On the great stage of supreme wisdom," that is to say, in the whole of nature, it would be precisely "in that part [of nature] which above all [others] contains its aim—the history of the human species," that this cruel seduction would take place!

The critical judge, guardian of the practical interests of reason, must be susceptible to this indignation. He convokes both parties: the one who says that human history is simply disorder, and the one who says it is organized by a providential nature. He explains to the former, as we have already heard: if you stick to cognitive phrases, and if you can provide examples and counterexamples for each phrase of this family, then you are legitimated in speaking of disorder, but only within the previously indicated limits proper to the family of cognitives in the matter of history. And with that you can make no more than a pragmatic politics, a politics of prudence, supported by the fact that, as the *Project for Perpetual Peace* explains, "history provides contradictory examples from all kinds of government [*Regierungsarte*]" (345). You would be but a "*political moralist*," and not a moral politician (*Project* 340ff.). He says to the other: you presuppose the Idea of a purposiveness in nature operating preeminently throughout the history of humanity and leading to a final end that only freedom can bring about (*KUK* 301ff.). You are then phrasing not according to the rule of direct presentation proper to cognitives but according to the free, analogical presentation to which dialectical phrases in general are beholden. You may therefore call on certain phenomena given in intuition; they cannot however have value in your argument as examples or schemata, but only as symbols, ideals, and other such signs. In linking them together, you will not obtain a law of mechanical or even organic development, but only a guiding thread. As explained in the *Critique of Judgment*, the guiding thread, which is reflective, takes nothing away from the subsumption of intuitions under concepts, that is, from the rule of the cognitive phrase. These are two heterogeneous, and compatible, phrase families. The same referent, a given phenomenon taken from the field of human history, may serve by way of example to present the object of the discourse of despair, but as a bit of guiding thread, it may also serve to present analogically the object of the discourse of emancipation. And with this guiding thread, you can pursue an analogically republican politics, and be a moral politician (*Project* 322–25).

The other expression—that of *sign of history*—introduces a further degree of complexity into the "passages" that are needed to phrase the historico-political. The question raised (in the Conflict with the Faculty of Law, I remind you) is whether it can be asserted that the human race is constantly progressing toward the better, and if so, how that can be affirmed. This question is also so far as we are concerned the one not raised (but only resolved) in the *Idea* of 1784: whether there exist "natural dispositions in the human species which are in affinity with the use of reason." These dispositions are to be presented, not from the standpoint of a transcendental subject of knowledge or morality, but within that zoological entity that is the human species.

The first difficulty resides in the fact that we are dealing with a phrase whose referent is a part of human history that is yet to come, hence a phrase of *Vorhersagung*, of anticipation or prognostication. Kant distinguishes it right away from the phrase of the *Weissager* (of the sooth-sayer), by recalling that there cannot be (according to the rules for cogni-tives) any direct presentation of the object of this phrase since it bears on the future (even if, which is not to be excluded for Kant, it believes it has the means, that is, the power, to constrain ulterior facts in conformity with its vaticinations).

For the requested demonstration, it will be necessary to change phrase families. It will be necessary to seek in the experience of human-ity, not an intuitive datum (a *Gegebenes*), which can never do anything more than validate the phrase that describes it, but what Kant calls a *Begebenheit*, an event, an "act of delivering itself" ["*fait de se livrer*"] that would also be an act of deliverance [*fait de se délivrer*], the chance of a "draw" [*une "donne"*: in the card-playing sense—Trans.].⁶ This *Begebenheit* would merely indicate (*hinweisen*) and not prove (*beweisen*) that humanity is capable of being both cause (*Ursache*) and author (*Urheber*) of its progress. More precisely, explains Kant, this *Begebenheit* which delivers itself into human history must indicate a cause such that the occurrence of its effect remains undetermined (*unbestimmt*) with regard to time (*in Ansehung der Zeit*): we recognize the indepen-dence clause of a causality through freedom in relation to the various diachronic series of the mechanical world. This causality can intervene at any time (*irgendwann*, repeats the Crakow manuscript). For this is the price paid for being able to extend this cause's possibility of intervention into the past as well as into the future (*Conflict* 301f.).

And that's not all: the *Begebenheit* ought not to be in and of itself the cause of progress, but merely its index (*hindeutend*), a *Geschichtszeichen*. Kant right away specifies what he means by sign of history: "*signum rememorativum, demonstrativum, prognosticum.*" The sought-for *Begebenheit* would have the task of "presenting" causality through freedom according to the three temporal directions of past, present, future. What is this enigmatic, if not contradictory, "act of delivering itself"? We might expect some momentous deed to be the sought-for "draw" that attests to the power of free causality. A momentous deed is still only a datum. It certainly allows for several readings (the descriptive phrase, the dialectical phrase) as has previously been stated with regard to the *Idea*, but it is thereby just an equivocal object which may be grasped by one phrase or the other, indifferently. Here, what is required of the critical judge goes beyond mere conciliation, to the point of appearing paradoxical. It is not sufficient for him to dismiss both the advocate of determinism and the advocate of freedom thanks to an arrangement that satisfies both, but rather he constrains them together and positively to exercise joint sovereignty over the sought-for event. If not given *by* experience, then at least given *in* experience, or "delivered," the *Begebenheit* ought to be the index, probative as it were (we shall see) of the Idea of free causality. With it, one must come right up to the edge of the abyss to be crossed between mechanism and freedom or purposiveness, between the domain of the sensible world and the field of the supersensible, and one must be able to cross it with a single step without suppressing it, by fixing the status of the historico-political, inconsistent, indeterminate perhaps, but utterable and even probative as it may be. This is the price paid for being able to prove that the natural disposition of humanity to make use of speculative reason can in effect be realized, and that one can anticipate, without fear of error, a continuous progress toward the better in its history.

Kant then takes what might appear to be an unexpected detour to present the said *Begebenheit*, but this detour will also allow for the "as-if" object that is the historico-political to be pinpointed with the most minute calibration and with the greatest fidelity to its complexity. We have an event, he writes, which satisfies the givens of the problem. It is not at all a momentous deed; it is not the revolution,

it is simply the mode of thinking [*Denkungsart*] of the spectators [*Zuschauer*] which betrays itself [*sich verrät*, as one *betrays* a secret] *publicly* [*öffentlich*, hence in a public use of thought, in the sense given, as we shall see, by the article on *Aufklärung*, which distinguishes a public use of reason] when it is a matter of [so I translate "*bei*," and not as "*in*"] this game of great upheavals [*Umwandlungen*] [this game, *dieses Spiel*, which one? The example he will give is that of the French Revolution, the text being from 1795]; for there is expressed on behalf of the players on the one side against those on the other, a taking of position [a taking in charge, *une prise en charge*, *eine Teilnehmung*] that is so universal and yet so devoid of personal interest—even at the risk that this position-taking may be very disadvantageous to them [the spectators]—that it reveals [*beweist*, "proves"], at least in its predisposition [*Anlage*], a character common to the human race as a whole (by reason of its universality) and a moral character [*moralisch*] (by reason of its disinterestedness), and this character not only permits people to hope for progress toward the better, but it is already that [this progress], within the limits that the present ascribes to the capacity for progress. (*Conflict* 302)

Kant adds that the recent revolution of a "*geistreich*" people, one rich in spirit, that is, may well fail or succeed, it may accumulate misery and atrocities, but "it [the French Revolution] nonetheless finds in the hearts [*in den Gemütern*, in the minds, in the sense that we speak of *putting minds at ease*] of all spectators (who are not directly engaged in this game themselves), a *position taking* [a participation] based in desire [*eine Teilnehmung dem Wunsche nach*] which borders closely on enthusiasm [*Enthusiasmus*] and which, since its very exteriorization is fraught with danger, can therefore have no other cause than a moral predisposition in the human race" (*Conflict* 302).

I will not offer a detailed commentary of a text, in which is compressed and even condensed Kant's thinking—perhaps all of Kant's thinking—on the historico-political. I will content myself with three observations, one on the nature of enthusiasm, another on its value as *Begebenheit* in the historical experience of humanity, the third on its

relation to the critic. All three will proceed under the clause that domi-
nates the elaboration of the *sign of history*, namely that "the sense" of
history (that is to say, all the phrases that are pertinent for the historico-
political field), does not take place solely on the stage of history, amid the
great deeds and misdeeds of the agents or actors who illustrate them but
also in the feelings of obscure and distant spectators (the theater hall of
history) who watch and hear them, and who make distinctions between
what is just and what is not in the sound and the fury of the *res gestae*.

   First observation. The enthusiasm they experience is, according to
Kant, a modality of the sublime feeling. I say *sublime feeling* rather than
feeling *of the* sublime (and it is the whole question of the "as-if" object
that I broach by this) since, if we are to believe the third *Critique*, "it is
the disposition of the mind resulting from a certain representation that
occupies the reflective judgment, but not the object, which is to be called
sublime" (*KUK* 134). The imagination tries to supply an object given in
a whole of the intuition, that is, to supply a presentation for an Idea of
reason (for the whole is the object of an Idea, for example the whole of
practical reasonable beings), it does not achieve this, it thereby experiences its inadequacy, but at the same time it discovers its destination
(*Bestimmung*, calling), which is to bring itself into accord with the Ideas
of reason through a suitable presentation. It results from this contraried
relation that instead of experiencing a feeling for the object, one experiences on the occasion of this object a feeling "for the Idea of humanity
in ourselves as subjects" (*KUK* 141). In the text of § 25, the feeling com-
mented on by Kant is that of respect. But the analysis holds for every
sublime feeling insofar as it entails a "subreption," the substitution of a
reconciliation (that is a nonreconciliation) between the faculties within a
subject for a reconciliation between an object and a subject.

   It should be noted that this demand to bring back the question of
the "passage" that is raised by aesthetic presentation, and in particular
by that one corresponding to the sublime, to the inwardness of a subject
in the reflective mode does not prevent Kant from speaking constantly
about the sublime as an object, for instance in the following "description": the sublime is "an object (of nature) *which prepares the mind to
think the impossibility of attaining nature regarded as a presentation of
Ideas*" (*KUK* 151). This is a point of hesitation only for a philosophy that

would decide a split with no possibility of appeal between what belongs to the subject and what belongs to the object. But for critique, the object is in general what can be presented in a given phrase family with a view to its validation, and when it is a matter of aesthetic phrases, this object can only be indirectly presentable, through an analogical procedure that is seated in the subject. The reflexivity of the judgment in this case (and in others) underscores the importance of the rule, be it free, of appropriate presentation. In this sense, the object is no longer anything more than the occasion to revisit the regulation.

The regulating of the sublime is a nonregulating. Unlike taste, the regulating of the sublime is good when it is bad. The sublime entails the purposiveness of a nonpurposiveness and the pleasure of a displeasure: "We find a certain purposiveness in the displeasure felt with regard to the necessary extension of the imagination in order to accord with that which is unbounded in our faculty of reason, viz. the Idea of the absolute whole, and consequently in the nonpurposiveness [*Unzweckmässigkeit*, a nonaffinity or incommensurability with regard to aim] of the power of the imagination for Ideas of reason and for their arousal [*Erweckung*]. . . . The object is grasped as sublime with a joy that is possible only through the mediation of a pain" (*KUK* 143).

The imagination, even at its most extended, does not succeed in presenting an object that might validate or "realize" the Idea. Whence the pain: the incapacity to present. What is the joy that is nonetheless grafted onto this pain? It is the joy of discovering an affinity within this discordance: even what is presented as really big, nature (including human nature, and the natural history of man, such as a great revolution) is still and always will be "small in comparison with" the Ideas of reason (*KUK* 141). What is discovered is not only the infinite import of Ideas, incommensurable to all presentation, but also the destination of the subject, "our" destination, which is to supply a presentation for the unpresentable, and therefore, with regard to Ideas, to exceed everything that can be presented.

Enthusiasm, in its turn, is an extreme mode of the sublime: the attempt at presentation not only fails, arousing the said tension, but it reverses itself, so to speak, or inverts itself in order to supply a supremely paradoxical presentation, which Kant calls "a merely negative presentation," a kind of "abstraction," and which he boldly characterizes as a "presentation of the infinite" (*KUK* 156). What we have here is the most inconsistent possible "passage," the impasse as "passage." Kant is even emboldened to give some examples of it: "Perhaps there is no more sublime passage (*Stelle*) in the Old Testament than the commandment: 'Thou shalt not make unto thyself any graven image, or any likeness of anything that is in heaven, or in the earth, or under the earth,' etc. This commandment alone can explain the enthusiasm that the Jewish people felt in its civilized period for its religion, when it compared itself with other peoples, or the pride that Mohammedanism inspired." And he goes on, "The very same thing also holds for the representation of the moral law and of the predisposition to morality in us" (*KUK* 156ff.). (This is the place to remember what this enthusiasm aroused by abstraction will become under the pen of the young Hegel, sketching out "the spirit of Judaism" seven or eight years later in Frankfurt: the mark of slavery, the realization of ugliness, a trace of animal existence. . . . All of this explicitly attributed by the same stroke to Kantianism.)

What is required for this abstract presentation, which presents nothingness, is that the imagination be "unbounded" ["*s'illimite*"] (*unbegrenzt*). (This would be a good point of departure for a philosophy of abstract art. If the aesthetics of Romanticism is certainly linked to the philosophy of the sublime, so-called abstract art would be its most radical emanation and perhaps its exit route. At the opposite pole, we should not be surprised to find Kojève trying to thematize it in Hegelian fashion in a little text called "Pourquoi concret," about Kandinsky's early Abstractions.[7])

There remains the fact that this extremely painful joy that is enthusiasm is an *Affekt*, a strong affection, and as such it is blind and cannot therefore, writes Kant, "merit a satisfaction [*un satisfecit, ein Wohlgefallen*] of reason" (*KUK* 154). It is even a *dementia*, a *Wahnsinn*, where the imagination is "unreined." As such, it is certainly preferable to *Schwärmerei* [fanaticism], to the tumultuousness of exaltation, which is a *Wahnsinn*, an *insanitas*, an "unruledness" ["*dérèglement*"] of the imagination, an "illness deep-rooted in the soul," whereas enthusiasm is "a passing accident, which can affect the most healthy understanding." The *Schwärmerei* is accompanied by an illusion: "*seeing something beyond all bounds of sensibility*" (*KUK* 156–57), that is, believing there is a direct presentation when there isn't any; it proceeds to a noncritical passage, comparable to the transcendental illusion (cognizing something beyond all bounds of cognition). Enthusiasm, for its sake, sees nothing, or rather sees nothingness and relates it back to the unpresentable. Although ethically condemnable as pathological, "aesthetically, enthusiasm is sublime, because it is a stretching of the powers through Ideas, which give the mind a momentum that acts far more powerfully and persistently than the impetus given by sensory representations" (*KUK* 154–55).

Historico-political enthusiasm is thus on the verge of dementia; it is a pathological outburst, and as such it has in itself no ethical validity, since ethics requires freedom from any motivating pathos; ethics allows only that apathetic pathos accompanying obligation that is respect, if not the all-too-sublime *Affektlosigkeit* onto which Kant links right away in the study of the sublime (*KUK* 154). In its episodic unleashing, however, enthusiastic pathos conserves an aesthetic validity; it is an energetic *sign*, a tensor of *Wunsch*. The infinity of the Idea draws to itself all the other capacities, that is, all the other faculties, and produces an *Affekt* "*of the vigorous kind*" (*KUK* 154), characteristic of the sublime. As can be seen, the "passage" does not take place; it is a "passage" in the course of coming to pass [*en train de se passer*], and its course [*son train*], its motion, is a kind of agitation in place, within the impasse of incommensurability, over the abyss, a "vibration [*ébranlement*]" as Kant writes, that is, "a rapidly alternating repulsion from and attraction to one and the same object" (141). Such is the state of *Gemüt* for the spectators of the French Revolution.

Second observation. This enthusiasm is the *Begebenheit* that has been sought for within the historical experience of humanity so as to be able to validate the phrase: "Humanity is constantly progressing toward the better." Great mutations, like the French Revolution, are not, in principle, sublime by themselves. As object, they are similar to those spectacles of (physical) nature on whose occasion the viewer experiences the sublime: "It is mostly rather, if only it allows a glimpse of magnitude and might, in its chaos and disorder, in its wildest and most unruly havoc, that nature best excites the ideas of the sublime" (*KUK* 130). What best determines the sublime is what is undetermined, the *Formlosigkeit* (*KUK*

130); "the sublime in nature . . . can be considered as entirely formless and shapeless" (*KUK* 160); "no particular form is represented in nature" (*KUK* 130). The same ought to apply thereby for the revolution, and for all great historical upheavals: they are formless and shapeless in the history of human nature. Ethically, they are nothing that can be validated; they fall on the contrary under the sway of critical judgment, and, as we have seen, they result from a confusion, which is the political illusion itself, between the direct presentation of the phenomenon of the *gemeines Wesen* and the analogical presentation of the Idea of the republican contract.

Insofar as it is an event in the natural history of humanity, the revolution belongs to that residue of data, to that remainder of singularities and existences that waits to be phrased once the cognitive phrase has taken charge of, by way of the presentation of examples, what belongs to it in the intuitions it is able to subsume under regularities. This remainder awaits the teleological phrase, and nonetheless its lack of form would appear to oblige it to fail absolutely. But in the enthusiasm this "formlessness" arouses in the *Gemüt* of spectators, this failure of every possible purposiveness is itself rendered purposeful. The dementia of enthusiasm with regard to the revolution and in favor of the revolutionary party testifies to the extreme tension spectating humanity experiences between the "nullity" of what is presented to it and the Ideas of reason, that is to say, in this case the Idea of republic that conjoins that of the autonomy of the people with that of peace among States (*Conflict* 302). What is delivered in this *Begebenheit* is thus a tension of the *Denkungsart* on the occasion of an object that is almost pure disorder, which is devoid of figure, which is really big however in historical nature, which is something abstract, rebellious to any function or presentation, be it analogical. But on account of these negative properties of the object that provide the occasion for this tension, it only proves even more indubitably, by the very form it impresses on feeling, that it is polarized "*auf Idealische*, toward something Ideal, *und zwar rein Moralische*, that is, something purely moral, such as," Kant adds, "the concept of right" (*Conflict* 303).

We understand why the *Begebenheit*, which ought to make a sign of history, could be found only on the side of the audience watching the spectacle of the upheavals. On stage, among the actors themselves, interests, ordinary passions, and the whole pathos of empirical (psychical, sociological) causality can never be extricated from the interests of pure moral reason and the appeal of the Idea of republican right. The spectators, sitting on other national stages, which make up the theater hall for the spectacle, and where absolutism generally reigns, cannot on the contrary be suspected of having empirical interests in making their sympathies public (*öffentlich*), they even run the risk of suffering repression at the hands of their governments. That itself guarantees the—at least aesthetic—value of their feelings. It must be said of their enthusiasm that it is an aesthetic analog of pure, republican fervor, as the sublime is a symbol of the good.

To this is added a second argument in the audience's favor. It may be that the revolutionaries' action aims not only at the political constitution of France under the authority of the sole legitimate sovereign *de jure*, namely the people, but also at the federation of states in a project for peace, which then concerns the whole of humanity. It does not matter that their action remains localized on the French scene, and that, as Kant writes, the foreign spectators watch it "without the least view to taking an active part in it [*ohne die mindeste Absicht der Mitwirkung*]" (*Conflict* 303). (We know that this reservation is such that the Idea of the sovereignty of peoples and of their peaceful federation would have to be realized, or fail to be realized, by means of war.) *Teilnehmung* through desire is not a participation in the act. But it is worth more. The sublime feeling, for its sake, is in fact spread out onto every scene on every national stage, and potentially at least, it is immediately universal. It is not universal the way a well-formed and validated cognitive phrase can be; a judgment of cognition has its determining rules set "before it," while the sublime phrase judges in the absence of rules. But, like the phrase of taste (the feeling of the beautiful), it does have an a priori that is not a rule that is already universally recognized, but a rule in waiting, a rule with the "promise" of universality. It is this universality in abeyance [*en souffrance*] that is invoked by the aesthetic judgment. If it is to be legitimate, it requires the principle of a *sensus communis*, that is to say, writes Kant, "the Idea of a *gemeinschaftlichein Sinn*, of a communitarian sense" (*KUK* 173). He specifies this as "a faculty for judging that in its [aesthetic] reflection, takes account (a priori) of everyone else's mode of representation" (*KUK*). This common or communitarian sense does not guarantee that "everyone *will* assent [*übereinstimmen*] to my judgment, but that everyone *ought* to *consent* to it [*zusammenstimmen*]" (*KUK* 123). It is merely an "ideal norm," an "indeterminate norm" (*KUK* 123–24ff.). If the enthusiasm of the spectators is a probative *Begebenheit* for the phrase that says that humanity is progressing toward the better, it is because enthusiasm, as a pure aesthetic feeling, requires a common sense, it calls upon a "consensus" that is nothing more than a *sensus* that is indeterminate though *de jure*; it is an immediate and singular anticipation of a sentimental republic.

Third observation. This consensus invoked by the sublime feeling (as with taste, but with a difference to which we need to return) puts us right in the middle of the archipelago. The indeterminacy of this a priori "enjoined" universality in the aesthetic judgment is the trait thanks to which the antinomy of taste is solved in the Dialectic of the Aesthetical Judgment (*KUK* 213ff.). This judgment must not be based on concepts, for otherwise they could be disputed—so observes the thesis; it must be based on concepts, for otherwise we could not even discuss whether it can lay claim to universality—retorts the antithesis. This antinomy is solved by introducing the notion of a concept "in itself indeterminate and at the same time indeterminable" (*KUK* 215). The phrase of cognition requires the presentation of a corresponding intuition: the concept is then determined by means of the presentation that suits it, namely the schemata. The phrase of aesthetic judgment, on the contrary, "cannot be determined by any intuition," "through it, nothing is known," "consequently, it allows *no proof to be presented* for the judgment of taste" (*KUK* 216). There is a transcendental appearance (a *Schein*) in the aesthetic phrase just as there is one in the speculative phrase, and there is a corresponding illusion, which is unavoidable but not insoluble (*KUK* 215ff.; 216–17). In its theoretical usage, the illusion consists in extending the validity of the cognitive beyond its determination of a phrase by intuitional presentation. In its aesthetical usage, the critical judge declares: the aesthetic phrase is par excellence the phrase of the faculty of presentation, but that it has no concept under which to subsume its sensible or imaginative intuition, it cannot therefore determine a domain, but only a field. Moreover, that field is only determined to a second degree, reflectively, so to speak: not by the commensurability between a presentation and a concept, but by the indeterminate affinity between the capacity for presenting and the capacity for conceptualizing. And, in the case of the sublime, this affinity includes within it the "nonaffinity" of the two capacities: we could then say that this belongs to a third degree of determination. But this affinity is an Idea, its object is not directly presentable. It results from this that the universality invoked by the beautiful and the sublime is merely an Idea of community, for which no proof, that is, no direct presentation, will ever be found, but only indirect presentations.

This takes nothing away from the rights of the cognitive phrase over the same objects as the aesthetic phrase. In the antinomy of taste, as in the solution to the dynamical antinomies of the first *Critique*, it is a question of constituting thesis and antithesis into paratheses. Kant writes in the third *Critique*: "The resolution of an antinomy amounts merely to the possibility that two apparently contradicting propositions do not in fact contradict each other, but can be compatible with each other, even if the explanation of the possibility of their concept exceeds our faculty of cognition" (*KUK* 216).

Notably caught up too in the parathetic solution of an antinomy are the addressors and addressees of the heterogeneous phrases in conflict. Their situation is in principle regulated, that is, subject to determination, according to the way the referent is presented by the phrase. Besides, that's what the Analytic of the first *Critique* established. But in certain cases, foremost that of the ethical phrase, only the situation of the addressee is regulated (and thereby even the situation of the referent since one property of that phrase is that the addressee must make the referent, the action prescribed by the imperative, exist), that of the addressor of the moral law remaining indeterminable. Even more different is the case of the aesthetic phrase: what regulates the situation of addressor and addressee is that it is not ruled by experience or objectification, since there is no determinable presentation of the referent or object. However, this nonregulating rule still calls on a possible and necessary agreement (exemplarily so) between the addressor of the aesthetic evaluation and the addressee on the occasion of a referent, which is directly presentable only as a phenomenon for cognition. There is thus between them a bond of "communicability" (*KUK* 176) that is not subject to the rule of presentation valid for cognitive phrases. This communicability of the feeling issuing from the forms in which the object is given is required "as if it were a duty," and taste is the mode of the reflective faculty that judges it a priori (*KUK*). The *sensus communis* is thus in aesthetics what the whole of practical, reasonable beings is in ethics, if we compare them together to the cognitive community. It founds an appeal to community carried out a priori and taking place without determination, without any concept subsuming a direct presentation. The ethical community, however, is mediated by a concept of reason, the Idea of freedom, while the aesthetic community of addressors and addressees of the phrase concerning the beautiful is immediately inscribed as a requirement of the feeling, inasmuch as that feeling is one that is a priori to be shared.

If now we want to describe this thereby "enjoined" consensus, that is, if we want to take it as a reference in a cognitive phrase, we fall into antinomy, for we are constrained by the rules of cognition to formulate it in a way contrary to its status, on account of the fact that every object presented to a cognitive phrase with a view to validating it must be presented by means of a schema that makes it conceptually determinable, while the community of addressors and addressees required in aesthetic feeling is not an object that is directly presentable. It is "merely" the object of an Idea, and one that signals itself, in this case, "merely" through feeling. The case of sublime feeling is even more different insofar as the status of the community is concerned. This community can no more be presented directly here than it could in the case of taste. But in contradistinction to taste, the communicability required by the sublime feeling does not need a community of sensibility or of imagination, but one of practical reason, of ethics. The addressee must be made to understand here that the measurelessness [*démesure*] of size and might in nature is as nothing compared to our moral destination, freedom. And the addressee, if the argument is to be understood, must have cultivated this Idea of freedom in oneself. That's why the sensibility of the sublime, fully aesthetic though it remains, can serve as an index of humanity's progress in ethical culture, that is to say, "toward the better."

Enthusiasm as "Begebenheit of our time" is phrased therefore following the apparently antinomic and simply parathetic rule of aesthetics.

And it is the most parathetic of aesthetics, that of the most extreme sublime. First of all, because the sublime is not only a disinterested pleasure and a universal without a concept, such as taste, but also because it entails a purposiveness of counterpurposiveness and a pleasure of pain, as opposed to the feeling of the beautiful whose purposiveness is without a purpose and whose pleasure is due to the free accord of the faculties with each other. With the sublime, Kant advances far into the parathetic, so much so that the solution to the aesthetic antinomy appears much more difficult in the case of the sublime than for the beautiful.

And all the more so when we are dealing with enthusiasm, which is at the furthest extremes of the sublime. Kant recognizes in effect that "the disposition of the mind to the feeling of the sublime requires *eine Empfänglichkeit* to Ideas [that the mind be susceptible with regard to Ideas, sensitive to Ideas]" (*KUK* 148). And further on, "The judgment on the sublime in nature [in human nature also, for that matter] requires a certain culture" (*KUK* 148–49), which is not to say that the judgment is produced by culture, for "it has its foundation in human nature." In this paragraph, Kant says nothing more on the subject. But this allusion to culture finds its elucidation in the paragraph of the Critique of Teleological Judgment that bears on the ultimate end of nature. There, Kant refutes, as he does in many of the shorter political works, the thesis that this end might be the happiness of the human race, and he demonstrates that it can only be its culture. "The production of the aptitude of a rational being for any ends that may please him (thus those of his freedom) is *culture*" (*KUK* 299). Culture is the ultimate end pursued by nature in the human race (as a part of nature, an eminent part of the "great stage of supreme wisdom") (*Idea* 119), because culture is what makes people more "susceptible to Ideas," it is the condition that opens onto the thought of the unconditioned.

In the same paragraph, Kant distinguishes between the culture of skill and the culture of will, and, within the former, between the material and the formal culture of skill. But this formal development of the culture of skill requires the neutralization of conflicts between freedoms, carried out on the level of individuals through a "legal power in a whole, which is called *bürgerliche Gesellschaft*, civil society," and if humans succeed in outpacing the plan of natural providence, then the development of the culture of skill requires the same neutralization, but this time on the level of states through "a cosmopolitan whole, *ein weltbürgerliches Ganzes* [world civil society]," which would be a federation of states (*KUK* 300).

In this way, the enthusiasm that publicly betrays itself on the occasion of the French Revolution, first because it is an extreme sublime feeling, then because this feeling already requires a formal culture of skill, and finally because this culture in turn has civil and perhaps international peace as its horizon—this enthusiasm by itself—"not only permits people to hope for progress toward the better, but is already itself progress insofar as its capacity is sufficient for the present" (*Conflict* 302).

So it is not just any aesthetic phrase, but that of the extreme sublime, which is able to display (*beweisen*) that humanity is constantly progressing toward the better. The beautiful is not sufficient; it is merely a symbol of the good. But, because the sublime is the sentimental paradox, the paradox of experiencing publicly and *de jure* as a group that something which is "formless" alludes to a beyond of experience, it constitutes an "as-if" presentation of the Idea of civil society and even of cosmopolitan society, and thus of the Idea of morality, right where that Idea nevertheless cannot be presented, within experience. This is the way in which the sublime is a sign. This sign is indicative only of a free causality, but it nonetheless has "proof" value for the phrase that affirms progress, since the spectating humanity must already have made cultural progress in order to be able to make this sign, by its "way of thinking" the revolution. This sign is progress in its present state; it is as much as can be done, even though civil societies are nowhere near republican in their regime nor states anywhere near world federation (far from it).

If this sign can be discerned by Kantian thought, it is because that thought is not just a reading but a component. The faculty of judgment at work in the critical thought of the *Conflict*, even if it is not of the same phrase family as the popular feeling that discerns the Idea of freedom in the historical datum that is the "French Revolution," is nonetheless made possible by the same progress in morality as that feeling. The sign in question is indicative at best when it is evaluated according to the standard of the presentational rule for phrases of historical cognition, a mere *Begebenheit* amid the *Gegebenheiten* that are intuitable historical data. But within the family of the strange phrases of judgment, this same sign is a proof for the Kantian phrase which judges that there is progress, since this sign is itself this (popular) phrase, certainly not "said," but publicly expressed as a feeling in principle able to be shared, and felt on the occasion of an "abstract" datum. Kant's "There is progress" does no more than reflect the peoples' "There is progress," which is necessarily implied in their enthusiasm.

So it is that Kant, with some solemnity, can link on as follows: "I claim at present that one can foretell [*vorhersagen*]—even without prophetic insight—according to the aspects and precursory signs [*Vorzeichen*] of our times, the attainment [*Erreichung*] of this end for the human race, and at the same time, along with that end, humanity's progress toward the better, which is henceforth no longer completely reversible. For, Kant adds, "such a phenomenon in human history *is no longer to be forgotten* [vergisst sich nicht mehr]" (*Conflict* 304). No politician (the politician of *politics* [*la* politique], the one Kant calls the "political moralist") could have been "shrewd enough to extract out of the course of things hitherto existing" this capacity for the better that enthusiasm has discovered in human nature. "In order to promise [*verheissen*] this," he adds, it would be necessary to have "nature and freedom reunited in the human race by the inner principles of right, but only in a undetermined way so far as time is concerned, and only as a *Begebenheit* coming along by chance" (*Conflict*). Untimeliness and fortuitousness show up to recall the necessarily determinately indeterminate character of the "passage" between nature (the revolution and the pathological aspect of the feeling it arouses) and freedom (the stretching toward the moral Idea of the absolute good, which is the other aspect of the same feeling). "There is progress": the critical judge can legitimate this phrase every time he is able to present a sign that serves as a referent for that assertion. But he cannot say when such objects will present themselves, the historical sequences that form series only give the historian data (statistically regular, at best) but never signs. The historico-political is presented to assertion only through cases, which operate not as examples and still less as schemata, but as complex hypotyposes (what Adorno demanded under the name of *Modelle*), the more complex ones being the surer. Popular enthusiasm for the revolution is a highly validating case for the historico-political phrase, thus allowing for a very sure hypotyposis, and this for a simple reason: that it is itself a highly improbable hypotyposis (recognizing the Idea of republic in a "formless," empirical datum). As for the philosophy of history, of which there can be no question in a critical thinking, it is an illusion born from the appearance that signs are examples or schemata.

Two Methods and One Manner of Phrasing the Historico-Political

According to Kant, "philosophizing," which is a "criticizing," that is, a "judging," is an analog of "politicking." Politics is no more something one can learn than philosophy, or else it is nothing more than a pragmatic prudence, that of the "political moralist," for whom Ideas are but a means and morality a technique. The politician, according to Kant, the ideal of political man, is the "moral politician" (*Project* 340). He must still judge as much as the "political moralist," but the latter thinks he holds a criterion for evaluating the "right" phrase case by case, and this criterion is that of well-being or advantage; it doesn't matter here whether it be that of the individual, the people, or the state. The moral politician has no criterion and is guided by the Idea of sovereign good, which is freedom as a legislative principle, and a decision must be rendered whether for a given prescriptive phrase, that is, a given maxim of the political will, one can present not directly the advantage that would result technically and pragmatically but indirectly, by means of the "as if it were the law of some nature," its compatibility with the ideal of a republican community. The "moral politician" is thereby engaged in a war of interests just like the critical philosopher in the war between Schools. In the *Proclamation of the Imminent Conclusion of a Treatise of*

Perpetual Peace in Philosophy, published in 1796, a year after the *Project for Perpetual Peace*, and with which Kant meant to put an end to his polemic with Schlosser, not only is the field of philosophy presented as a *Kampfplatz*, but what appeared only as an analogical narrative in the first Preface to the first *Critique* turns out at present to be legitimated as a symbolic, to be sure *indirect*, presentation of the polemical condition of precritical philosophy. There is, writes Kant, a *Hang*, a penchant to reason methodically, that is to say, to philosophize, a *Hang* to confront philosophical phrases, to "dispute" and "*squabble*," a *Hang* to cluster into Schools, in order to "*wage* open *warfare*," against one another, and this *Hang* is much more than an inclination; it is even a *Drang*, an urge, to fight in phrases (I would say: a drive for phrases to meet head-on).[1] This bellicose disposition is given the same indirect legitimation by the "as if" of a nature full of wisdom as what Kant proposed for the state of war between nations: the peace there that humans grouped into states, here philosophers gathered into Schools, cannot bring themselves to institute freely even though peace is nonetheless the condition for the development of free reason among all, all happens "as if" nature constrained them "despotically" (*Project* 333) to approach each other by means of war and commerce (material in the one case, and intellectual in the other).

When Kant "proclaims" the institution of philosophical peace, he does not mean to plunge thought into the "sleep of the dead" (*Proclamation* 455); he is referring to the institution of the critical tribunal, before which, as we read at the beginning of the first *Critique*, phrases present themselves no longer armed from head to toe with their validity, under the name of Schools, but offered to the critical examination that legitimates them according to the form that corresponds to the rule of the family to which each belongs and according to the mode of presentation that suits each. The battle is not over, and it will always go on because the power of Ideas is infinite, and because the republic as Idea is infinitely removed, but the field has been commuted (cultivated), "*war*" has become a "*lawsuit*" (*KRV* 623); it's the faculty of judgment and no longer (only) the urge of nature that exerts its power there. And, as we know, it judges not according to a determined criterion but according to an ideal, that of a philosophy that legislates human reason, that is, a philosophy sensitive to the essential ends of that reason.

It follows from this, first of all, that all the writings signed by Kant must themselves be political texts in the sense of a "moral politics." Second, it follows—by reason of the fact that these writings cannot supply direct presentations for the evaluation of their own phrases in terms of how calibrated they are to the end Idea of human reason—that they must arise from different phrase families, or even from concatenations of such diverse phrase families into genres of discourse that are themselves different. They must thereby constitute an archipelago of phrase families and genres of discourse that is analogous to the archipelago that constitutes the historico-political field. And in particular, when the philosopher takes this historico-political field as a referent or at least as the semantic theme of his own philosophical phrases, he must have a "choice," if one may say so, from among several ways to phrase that field. Considering the indeterminacy of the "passages" destined to present objects able to have value as "realities" in order to validate the philosophical phrase concerning the historico-political, it is to be expected that the "passages" borrowed by Kant would be of several sorts. We should then find a multiplicity of genres in Kant's texts on the historico-political, a multiplicity called forth by the determinately indeterminate nature of the play of the faculty of judgment in search of its guiding threads or its signs. Undoubtedly, the fragmentation of Kant's historico-political texts is commensurate with this demand for multiplicity. And this multiplicity is the point at which the question of the *style* of Kantian thought in these matters must be raised. Let me present three cases.

In the *Idea* of 1784, the title—Idea for a Universal History from a "Cosmopolitical" (that is to say, world citizenship) Point of View[2]—appears to indicate clearly the nature of the Kantian phrase. In announcing its belonging to the family of Ideas, the phrase limits its claims to validity, such that it can only be that validity suitable to argumentatives as has been judged in the Dialectic of the first *Critique*: a concept in its simply logical usage, with no intuition mediated by a scheme, thus with no cognitive value, but thus also subject in its use to the rule of contradictory argumentation. It is a matter of linking together the phrases of the understanding according to the rule of reasoning. A phrase in this family is judged to be established (a predicate correctly attributed to a propositional subject) on the sole condition that it be concluded by the mediation of a universal: it is sufficient that the case (Caius) enters into the condition (man) for it to be legitimately judged that Caius is mortal (*KRV* 399). There is also the matter of reasoning with a view to refuting the opposing thesis.

This antithetical mode is more particularly pertinent in the text of 1784 on account of the fact that we are dealing with an *allgemeine Geschichte*, that is to say, with a *whole* of the human historical series and with a perspective (*Absicht*) on that whole that grasps it as a world, *welt-bürgerliche*. The cosmopolitical is a part, an exceptionally eminent one if we recall, of the cosmological. There is no reason to be surprised, then, that the text of the *Idea* proceeds by means of *Sätze*, phrases with logical value, propositions, that are linked by logical operators with a view to refuting the antithesis of moroseness, of the *Unwillen*. Nor is there any reason to be surprised that, at the end of the *Idea*, Kant may appear to doubt the scope of his argumentation: "It is, to be sure, a strange project and one by all appearances without rhyme or reason [*ungereimt*] to want to put together [*abfassen*, to draw up a piece of writing] a *history* in accordance with an Idea of the course the world must take if it is to be commensurate [*angemessen*] with certain rational ends" (*Idea* 118). Moreover, there is no reason to be surprised that he is content to grant it a validity that would appear minor only to a reader who falls prey to the political illusion: "Nevertheless, this Idea could become useful [*wohl brauchbar*]."

The text that publicly argues the Idea of a universal history cannot be declared true or false, but it can be useful or useless. The use that is here invoked as a criterion of validity ought to be examined as it is in the third section of the Antinomy of Pure Reason, where the theses and antitheses of the Antithetic are judged according to the interest of reason. This interest breaks down into three aspects: practical, speculative, and popular (*KRV* 498ff.), which correspond respectively to the domain of ethics, the field of the theoretical (dialectics), and the field of the political. To follow Kant's conclusions in the first *Critique*, we can affirm that the thesis of a cosmopolitical purposiveness to universal history presents a practical and popular interest. As for speculative interest, for which the empirical antithesis in the first *Critique* sees a great advantage ceded to it over its dogmatic adversary (on the condition that empiricism itself does not fall into dogmatism), it appears assured that the *Idea for a Universal History* is equally the beneficiary, since it clearly exposes, just as empiricism would, that "all that our Ideas make known to us really is *that we know nothing*" (*KRV* 500), and that the dialectical phrase must not be confused with a phrase of science. It is thereby altogether proper for awakening the mind and keeping it awake, and in this way, it is in effect "full of use" (*Idea* 118).

The evaluation of the utility of the Idea phrase singularly sheds light on one of the instances of this phrase: its addressee. A possible utility presupposes a possible utilizer, which is this addressee. What is the addressee, then, of these dialectical phrases exchanged in the politico-philosophical battle? The *Answer to the Question: What Is Enlightenment?* strongly circumscribes the field of the political critic's phrases, and thus their presumable effect on the addressee. This *Answer* is not, or not simply, a text argued in accordance with the Idea, but a text that at the same time (as is the case for the *Proclamation*) sets the rules for the conflict of Ideas within the historico-political field. It thus has the status of procedural regulation, particularly with regard to what touches on the addressee (the reader) of the historico-political works. Since the phrases that refer to this field are, by dint of their possible use, already themselves phrases within this field, that is to say, themselves events of historico-political thought, the question here is not really that of knowing which rules regulate their formation and legitimation, even if their occurrence within this field ought itself to be subject to procedural rules. The *ought* designates, as it almost always does in Kant, a limit of legitimacy to be found, in this case that of the occurrence of the moralist politician's phrase.

A public use (*öffentlich*) is distinguished from a private use (*Privatgebrauch*) of reason, the two usages being set in opposition by the canonical formula ascribed to Frederick the Great: "*Reason* as much as you will, and about what you will, *but obey!*"[3] Obeying is the "private" use of reason. The addressee of prescriptions, the one who is constrained by them, is here "a part of the [social] machine," a passive member of a "mechanism." The use of his reason must then be bounded by consideration for the interest of the *Gemeinwesen*, of the common being (*Idea* 18ff.). One ought not to argue about a command coming from an officer, about a taxation levied by the treasury, and also, if you happen to be a priest, about a symbol of the church one serves. One ought not to argue, unless it is to incur the greatest risk to the *Gemeinwesen*, the army, the treasury, the church: that of its dissolution. For there is no right that gives anybody the authority to dissolve the social machine such as it is. We have previously heard why.

In return, considered *als Gelehrter*, as learned human being, everyone "assuredly" has the right, and even the duty, to argue about institutions, to "reason" (*freilich räsonnieren*) (*Idea*), in accordance with one's own understanding or reason, as a "free thinker" (*Idea* 22). What is in play, then, is not directly, by intuitional presentation in the phenomenon, the interests of persistence for the common being, but *Aufklärung*, that is to say, the development of the capacity to explore Ideas and to supply them with a presentation (which will be an "as-if" presentation), and for as far as that can go. The development of this capacity for Ideas, what the *Critique of Judgment* calls susceptibility or sensitivity to Ideas, a development that is nothing other than culture, is, writes Kant, "the sacred right of humankind" (*Idea* 20). No one has the authority to violate it, that is, to impede the free publication of Idea phrases. That, writes Kant, is "absolutely forbidden" (*Idea* 20).

Here, Kant's argument employs the major "as if" of his philosophy of authority: "The touchstone [*der Probierstein*, that is to say, the mode of presentation pertinent in these matters] of whatever can be decided as law for a people lies in the question: whether a people could indeed [*wohl*] impose such a law on itself?" The "passage" borrowed here by critical thought is to act "as if the republic were realized." For, critical thought finds that it is "contradictory" (the decisive formal criterion when it is a question of the correct formulation of dialectical arguments) that a people, as a set of reasonable beings, would be opposed to the development of the Ideas of reason (*Idea* 20).

This judgment is sufficient to determine the addressee of dialectical phrases in which the Ideas are developed as much as they can be. It's a "*Leserwelt*," writes Kant, a "world of readers" (*Idea* 18). If discussion is public, then it must be published, so that it can be read. Writing here allows us to dissociate between a world of readers, which insofar as it is a world is the object of an Idea (that of the set of reasonable beings), and a "common being" which, even if it is not properly speaking an intuitional given insofar as it requires the Idea of an organic purposiveness in order to be thought, does not fail for that matter to supply all kinds of phenomena subsumable under the scientific or teleological category of reciprocal action. Common being is at best the object corresponding to an objective, material purposiveness; the world of readers for its sake calls upon the Idea of an ethical, formal purposiveness, that of the free republic. The unification of these objects is not determinable by a direct presentation, for it is itself the object of an Idea, the Idea of developing the capacity for ends in man as the final end of nature.[4] The movement of various peoples toward a republican constitution is an index of this, but this index is not a phenomenon; it is an indirect presentation of the validity of the supreme teleological phrase, and within the field opened up by this phrase.

If we stick with the phrase of the *Gemeinwesen*, there is no index at all, and that is why learned persons, philosophers, free thinkers, even though they are "the natural heralds and expositors of natural rights among the people," do not address the people directly, do not address them *"vertraulich*, confidentially" (*Conflict* 148–49)—which is to say: that people, who then is not the potential *Leserwelt* within the field opened up by the ethico-political phrase, but only the common being to which the sociological or organicist phrase refers. But it is precisely because the phenomenal people is *not* the noumenal people that the philosopher *must* be able to publish his argument of Ideas, so that it can become that as much as possible. In this, the philosopher conforms to his Ideal as thinker of the world, and hence to the supreme ends of human reason. His reader as world is not yet there, but keeps on arriving, with every new published argumentation. And this, the power in charge must allow and facilitate, without intervening in the content itself of the exchanged Ideas and argumentations (*Answer* 21ff.; *TP* 302–3).

I cannot even hope to sketch out here a description of the various phrase families and various genres of discourse from which Kant's different historico-political writings arise. I would nonetheless like to come back to a word invoked at the end of the *Idea* of 1784 as an objection to the value of that writing. The latter, it may be recalled, appears to have neither rhyme nor reason; it remakes history as if it were measurable in terms of certain rational goals. "It appears," writes Kant, "that, within such a perspective, only a *novel* could be brought about" (*Idea* 118). This hypothesis, that after all the *Idea* may be nothing more than a novel, is not refuted, Kant links on to it by the argument that, in any case, it is useful. Can it be thought that, from among the various phrase families that have to take the historico-political archipelago into account, the literary phrase, the poetic one in the Aristotelian sense, the one belonging to the novelistic genre (which itself is not Aristotelian), turns out to be granted a legitimate place in its genre by the critical judge? In the remark from the *Idea* I've just recalled, this supposition appears to have been abandoned. But the case is more complicated than it appears.

First of all, where would the novelistic phrase find its place in the set of phrase families? In his division of the fine arts (*KUK* 197ff.), Kant depends on the simple opposition between poet and orator: the poet promises only a simple play of Ideas but provides a lot to think about; the orator promises to set the understanding to work, but through this use of rhetoric only gives rise to an entertaining play of the imagination (*KUK* 198ff.). The novel is not cited. It is cited in the General Remark on the Exposition of the Aesthetic Reflective Judgment (*KUK* 149ff.) in regard to *Affekte* of the vigorous kind, which aesthetically belong to the sublime. Contrary to vigorous ones tender emotions that, rising in intensity, become *Affekte*, never produce anything more than "sentimentality [*sensiblerie*]." Kant writes in regard to the latter that it "is not compatible with what can be counted on in beauty and still less with what can be considered as sublime in the soul's manner of being" (*KUK* 155). Now, what do we find in the works of sentimentality? "Novels, lachrymose plays, shallow moral precepts which toy with (falsely) so-called noble feelings, but which in fact make the heart unsympathetic and insensitive to the strenuous rule of duty and incapable of all respect for the worth of humanity in our own person, for the rights of humans (a very different thing from their happiness), and in a general way, incapable of respect for all firm principles" (*KUK* 155). The novel is condemned because it does not cultivate the will by showing the greatness of the obstacles that nature, as if it were following a plan, places before the realization of our empirical ends, the better to destine us to our ethical end. The addressee of such a novel, be it the novel of history, is not enlightened by what is read, nor does that addressee even experience that *Affekt* which is the sign of the presence of the Idea of reason being incommensurable with all presentation, and which is the sublime, or rather enthusiasm.

In relation to the notion of the ideal, there is found in the Dialectic of the first *Critique* (*KRV* 551ff.) a condemnation of the novel that sharpens the one we just read. The ideal, as we know, is that which, in the form of a prototypic individual, allows for the complete determination of the copy of an Idea. "Virtue, and along with it human wisdom in its entire purity, are Ideas. But the sage (of the Stoics) is an ideal." Does this come down to a presentation of the object of the Idea? Yes, it is not "a chimera," but it does not come from the family of examples, because there are no examples for Ideas. Kant then links on as follows: "But to try to realize [*realisieren*] the ideal in an example, that is, within phenomena, such as that of the sage in a novel, is not feasible, and even has about it something by itself absurd [*Widersinnisches,* that which goes against sense], and not very edifying [*wenig Erbauliches*], since the natural limits, which continually breach the perfection of the Idea, in effect render impossible every illusion in an attempt of this genre [the novel exemplifying an ideal], and thereby cast suspicion on the good that dwells within the Idea, leading us to regard it as a mere fiction [*eine blosse Erdichtung*]" (*KRV* 552ff.).

A double critique: the attempt to romance the ideal is absurd since an example is given within phenomena of something that cannot properly be "realized"; it cannot fulfill its goal of edification, since the good is withdrawn from its status as the object of an Idea, turning it then into an object of fiction. If the *Idea* of 1784 were a novel, it would succumb to a triple bill of accusations for sentimentality, incoherence, and demoralization. The novelistic phrase of the historico-political thus appears excluded from the archipelago, the "passage" between ideas in play and the presentations the phrase supplies is judged to be illegitimate by the critique, and by the same stroke, it is judged to be dangerous also in its effect on the addressee. There does perhaps exist, however, one recourse for the advocate of the novel. The term *Idea* in the title of the 1784 article has been interpreted in the sense of an Idea of reason. Does this exclude its being an Idea of the imagination?

The latter is opposed to the former as the extending of presentation without the possibility of a concept is opposed to the extending of the concept without the possibility of intuitional presentation (*KUK* 193, 217–18). The Idea of the imagination is a "representation of the imagination that occasions much thinking, without however any determined thought, that is, any *concept*, being capable of being adequate to it; and consequently, which no language can completely express and make intelligible" (*KUK* 192). The Idea of reason is "indemonstrable" in the sense that *demonstrieren* (*ostendere, exhibere*) signifies "to present its concept at the same time in intuition." The Idea of the imagination for its sake is "inexponible" in the sense that *exponieren* is "to bring a representation of the imagination to concepts" (*KUK* 218–19). A double impasse, it would seem, for the faculty of "passages." But we know that there are for Ideas of the reason, if not "demonstrations" properly called, at least indirect presentations of "as-if" objects, and of several sorts. Can we locate transactions of the same sort in the opposite direction when it is a matter of conceptually phrasing an overabundance of intuitions given by the imagination?

The aesthetic Idea is the affair of genius: genius is "the faculty of *aesthetic Ideas*" (*KUK* 219). The imagination, within the functioning of genius, furnishes unsought "over and above that agreement with a concept, a rich and undeveloped material for the understanding, of which the understanding took no regard in its concept" (*KUK* 194). For, is genius, this "favorite of nature" (*KUK* 196), not what is invoked at the beginning of the *Idea* of 1784 in order to write the history of humanity? "We are going to see," it is written there, "if it is possible for us to find a guiding thread for such a history; then we will leave to Nature the care to produce [*hervorbringen*] someone capable of writing [this history] following this thread. So it is," adds Kant, "that Nature produced *Kepler*, who subjected, in an unexpected way, the eccentric paths of the planets to determined laws, and she produced *Newton*, who explained these laws by a general principle of nature" (*Idea* 109ff.). Kepler and Newton should not be able to be geniuses following the definition offered in the third *Critique* ("it is a talent for art, not for science") (*KUK* 195), but if the Idea of universal history is an Idea of the imagination, the Keplers or the Newtons who compose the novel of this history in accordance with that Idea must be geniuses. They do not "exposit" that Idea; they show it without bringing it back to a concept.

The data supplied by history and reworked without rule by the imagination hand over to the novelistic phrase a material of such abundance that it is easy to judge that the understanding turns out to be overwhelmed and is never done thinking through this material. What was called, from the standpoint of the Idea of reason, the "nothingness" of historical disorder, a merely negative presentation, becomes, in the eyes of the critical judge who examines it from the perspective of the Idea of the imagination (that is to say, of the phrase of art), the overabundance, the profuseness of what ceaselessly presents itself and of what cannot find exposition in the cognitive phrase. To indicate (vainly) the "passage" in this sense, that is, going from artistic presentation to cognitive phrase, there is genius, but that is a gift of nature, to which we must leave the task of indicating this passage. We can reasonably hope that it will take up that task, in accordance with the Idea of a nature about which it would be all too painful to think that it could furnish so great a wealth of data with historical material without at the same time furnishing the capacity to phrase with the means to "demonstrate" that data.

Genius, we see, is the name of a "passage," and not one of the easiest, since it is forbidden: that passage that ought to lead from the family of the innumerable phrases of human experience to that of their unification under a concept of reason, in other words, the dialectical phrase. It is a passage analogous to the one described with regard to enthusiasm, where the ideal, transcendent sense of a datum, abstract by dint of being senseless, is signaled by the feeling. But with genius, the datum has become too concrete, and the Idea is what must be produced, that is to say, what will make the signal. In enthusiasm, humans are the addressees of an Idea they exhibit on the occasion of something that is almost nothing; in genius, they are the addressees of something that is much too much which can only be explained as an almost concept. That nature supplies this material in human experience and produces along with genius the impasse "passage" that would unify it in view of an Idea, that is in the eyes of the critical judge an Idea that is itself as legitimate as an Idea can be, and in which free thought surely locates its interests. So much so that, within these limits, the novelistic phrase ought to be able to be a legitimate fashion—as *"manner"* and not as *"method"* (*KUK* 196)—to phrase the historico-political.

It's in this light, it would seem, that we could understand, or at least close in on, the strange "manner" in which is written the text published in 1786 in the *Berlinische Monatschrift* and titled word for word: *Conjectural Beginning of Human History, Mutmasslicher Anfang der Menschengeschicte*. The study's exordium is explicit: it is permissible to introduce conjectures into the progression of a history in order to fill gaps in the available information. "But," writes Kant, *"to erect* an entire history upon conjectures does not seem much better than to make a draft [*Entwurf*] for a novel" (*Conjecture* 163). That history, he adds, "could not bear the name of *conjectural history*, but rather that of a *mere fiction* [*einer blossen Erdichtung*, the same expression as in the first *Critique*]." That draft of a novel is permitted, however, declares the critical judge, when dealing with the very first beginnings of history insofar as nature alone is in play, and not freedom. For the phrase that recounts these beginnings, in making reference to supposedly natural data (it's a matter of the nature of man), is not pure divagation, it relies on an "as-if" experience, inasmuch as it is presupposed that human nature in its earliest beginnings was no different, neither better nor worse, than it is today in our intuitionally presentable experience. Such a presupposition of the permanence of natural experience is legitimate even with regard to the understanding, and, writes Kant, it "conforms to the analogy of nature" (*Conjecture*). (I'm presuming here, without swearing to it, that we are dealing with the First Analogy of Experience, the principle of permanence of substance, extended to the Idea of nature.) (*KRV* 299ff.) At the beginning of the series of phenomena that constitute the history of humanity, things would be just as they are in the sequences of this series for which we do have intuitions.

Despite this support from theoretical reason the critical judge grants to the conjectural phrase, he is not bent on confounding it with the cognitive phrase: "Conjectures do not have the right to make excessively high claims on *Beistimmung*, on one's assent; they should at most announce themselves, not as really serious business, but as a movement [a *Bewegung, cheminement*, a traveling] conceded to the imagination in the company [*Begleitung*] of reason, for the sake of relaxation and the health of the *Gemüt*" (*Conjecture* 163ff.). The phrase of the conjectural text is thus under the rule of the Idea of imagination, but the understanding or reason throws in the cognitive regulation of the analogy of nature, and finally what is at stake on the addressee's side is not the supplying of a cognition, nor even an argumentation of the Idea, but a better state of the soul.

This last aspect is clearly underscored by the text's first addressee, namely its author: "I am venturing here," he writes, "on a mere pleasure trip [*Lustreise*], and I ask that I be granted the favor [he has already granted it to himself] of using a sacred text as my map. The course of my travel is carried out on the wings of the imagination, but not without a guiding thread attached by reason onto experience, and this course exactly follows the same track [*Linie*] as the historic one that text already contains inscribed within it" (*Conjecture* 163–64).

The addressee thereby solicited is not the *Leserwelt* partner, a free reason ready to link onto a speculative argument by means of refutation. The addressee is, first of all, asked to refer to the biblical text of Genesis and to accept that text as a cartographical symbol for the outline of a novel. The addressee is further asked to admit, as addressee of the cognitive phrase, the analogy of nature with itself. Finally, the addressee is asked to be in need of comforting.

What comforting? In the Concluding Remark to the *Conjecture*, Kant emphasizes this aspect. The conclusion in effect begins with these solemn words: "The thinking human being feels a sorrow [*einem Kummer*], one which can even become a moral corruption [a *Sittenverderbnis*, a perversion], of which the thoughtless [*un sans-pensée*] [*der Gedankenlose*] knows nothing" (173). The perversion that threatens thought in the face of the historico-political we have already identified as that of holding Providence, that is, the purposiveness of nature, in despair, and to accuse a world badly made as the cause of human misfortune. It is against this dangerous sorrow that "such a presentation of his history," as that of the *Conjecture*, brings to the thinking person "advantage and utility in the matter of one's instruction and improvement" (175). That person will see in effect that nature is not the cause of one's misfortune, but freedom, which nature has given him.

This phrase of conjecture thus offers a complex concatenation, in which the "passages" are multiple. First of all, a biblical text, which serves only as cartographic guide, the novelistic narrative marking its diegetic progress on this map step by step, assuring itself that it is following the correct directions. The sacred text is grasped, within the field of phrases of faith, which are received (that is, where the determinable instance is that of the addressee, the reader of the Bible) as an analog of the novelistic text within the field of phrases of the imagination, which are "invented" (where the determinable instance is that of the addressor, the writer who makes conjectures). Then, the sacred text is not itself the guiding thread, other signal of a "passage." This thread is provided by reason, as it ought to be; it is the symbol (taken from the experience of the labyrinth) of an Idea of purposiveness pursued by nature across the labyrinth of human history, even at its beginnings. Third, this thread, whose function is precisely that of traversing, remains attached to experience, since it is strung between it and the Idea of an end. This attachment is furnished by a judgment, that of analogy: as human nature was at its beginnings, so is it today, or the converse. Finally, the *Conjecture* belongs to the genre of the novel: it is a traveling of the imagination that gathers together without a concept the profusion of material from the natural experience of historical humanity, symbolically delivered up by the text of *Genesis* and analogically supposed by the conjectural narrative.

The outcome of this concatenation of heterogeneous phrases within a genre, the *Conjecture*, should bring about a comforting effect, which is properly ethical, on the addressee: touching down on a ground protected against depressing perversion. All the faculties are accounted for here. The biblical scenario is therein made "exponible" for the understanding, which there recognizes through analogy the regular sequences of acts or affects that constitute the domain of anthropological cognition. For its part, and in complete freedom and inventiveness, the imagination adds to this domain the new material, unforeseen by the understanding, which it finds in the Bible. The effect that results from all this is the pleasure given by the free play of the imagination in an unregulated, or at least not fully regulated, agreement with the faculty of cognition through concepts, hence a pleasure of beauty. Finally, reason organizes all these materials, those that are the objects of intuitional presentation

for the understanding, and those that the imagination seeks out in sacred legend, according to the Idea of an end pursued by nature within
humankind: driven out of Paradise, doomed to suffering, humankind
is also doomed to freedom. Such is the phrase of reason. Misfortune is
presented as a condition imposed by providence so that the species will
progress toward the better. The comfort comes from all these "passages"
being conjugated together: the biblical legend is intelligible, the disorder
referred to by the historian's phrase can be unified by the imagination,
this unity is arguable as an intelligent causality of nature.

Who is able to be convinced by such a machination of phrases?
But what is at stake in the *Conjecture* is not the convincing of the reader;
it is to give a reprieve from the fundamental sorrow of thinking about
history; it is to endow the *Gemüt* with a vigorous emotion, the only
moral passion, if we can say so. That passion is itself a passage from the
domain of pathology, which falls entirely under the rule for cognitive
phrases, where humankind is a referent, to the domain of ethics, which
the prescriptive phrase alone determines, and where humankind is the
addressee of an inscrutable addressor. This moral passion is that of the
"moral politician"; it is political *virtù*.

If there is a novel here, and there is some novel in the *Conjecture*,
even if it is not solely a novel, at least it does not sin through sentimentality. Surely, it is "sweet," writes Kant in a note to the *Conflict* with the
Faculty of Law, to forge utopias; they are "sweet dreams" that we have
the right to produce as such, and even that the head of state, but no one
else, has a duty to try to realize (*Conflict* 307n). But the phrase of the
Conjecture is not a utopian phrase, and its effect is not to soothe the sorrow that comes from the spectacle of history by substituting it with the
scene of a dreaming; it is to endow the reader with the vigorous *Affekt*.
It will be recalled that "every affection of the *vigorous* kind (viz. that
excites the consciousness of our power, to overcome all resistance) [*animi
strenui*] is *aesthetically sublime*" (*KUK* 154). As the Idea of the sublime
is analogous in the aesthetic phrase with the Idea of the Good in the
ethical phrase, so the vigorous affection is an analog, in the *Gemüt*, of
the affection for duty (which is not an affection) through the moral law,
the feeling of duty, respect. But respect is pure in the eyes of the critical
judge, at least in principle, while the vigorous affection must of necessity

be mixed, condemnable if brought back to the ethical phrase because
it is pathological, but legitimate according to the rules of the historico-
political phrase.

The *Conjecture* supplies an example (the text is given to us within
intuition) of judgment because it is made solely of interfaculty phrases.
Each of them gets a symbol for a name: map, guiding thread, *Bewegung*,
Lustreise. We sail in the archipelago, from the edge of one island to the
next, on the sea of the supersensible. We are immersed in the historico-
political without ever getting it as an object; we deal only with signs.
And the circuit of passages is legitimate, critically speaking, on the sole
condition that each of these signs is taken as such according to the het-
erogeneities it conjugates, or at least that it conjectures.

The addressee of the Kantian opuscule is cast into the thick of
politics, in the sense of "moral politics," for the text is placed under the
eminent consideration of the practical and popular interest of reason,
rather than its speculative interest. The addressee it institutes is not exactly the one proposed by the study on *Aufklärung*, a learned partner
ready to argue Ideas, in particular that of the purposiveness of history,
from a speculative viewpoint. Here, it is a partner to whom the power to
struggle must be rendered because that partner thinks, and in the thinking of history a disgust for history and the abandonment of thought
break through. The addressee must be torn from the perverse fascination
of indifferentism, of the "It's all the same," and even from the melancho-
lia of the "We don't matter." What must be rendered to the addressee is
the sublime humor the critical judge judges the addressee not only to be
capable of but that must be cultivated if it is true that is up to humans
alone, once nature has granted them the seeds and conditions for developing freedom, to realize that freedom: for if nature realized freedom in
their place, then freedom would be conditional, which is a contradiction. In the *Conjecture*, it is a matter of giving the addressee the capacity
for "passages," be it in the aesthetic "manner" rather than the logical
"mode," that is, the capacity to judge at work in the sublime feeling, as
the peoples who are spectators of the French Revolution will do. In 1786,
Frederick the Great will die; it will be necessary that the power to judge
justly, without criteria, be extended to the people, in order to resist the

return of the reaction, which brandishes the sacred text as its code. Such is the legitimately "edifying" destination of this outline of a novel.

In writing the *Conjecture*, the critical judge pronounces a verdict favorable in all respects to the claims raised by the novel to phrase the historico-political. The final condition for this favor is that it be a novel of culture, a *Bildungsroman*, in the critical sense of the cultivation of the will, for its protagonist and for its reader.

5

What Is Delivered in a Sentiment of Our Times

Three words in order . . . not to finish.

First word: the Kantian political seems to me as close as can be to what we understand today, crassly, as the political. The political experience of our time, utterly different from what Kant knew, proceeds in principle under the form of democracy, which is a *forma imperii, die Form der Beherrshung,* the manner in which domination is exerted (*Project* 324ff.). For Kant, this manner varies according to "the different persons who hold for themselves [*inne haben*] supreme State power." As for the manner in which the people are governed by the sovereign (*Oberhaupt*), the *Regierungsart* or *forma regiminis,* which is not immediately dependent on the form of domination, Kant distinguishes only two, the *republican* and the *despotic,* according to whether the state's principle is that of the separation, or not, between the executive power (the *Regierung*) and the legislative power. The stronger the separation, the less danger that the executive will be confused with the legislative, the less there is of a threat of despotism, which is the *Unform,* the form-less. The republic is brought closer to the extent that the two powers are kept apart: here again, the critical judge has as a first order of business that of splitting apart (*trancher*). What Kant calls representative (*repräsentativ*) is a disposition of the two powers such that the (unformed) confusion between them is in principle impossible.

Every noncritical "passage" from one to the other is illegitimate. Democracy is a case of political illusion, since it confuses to the greatest extent possible the capacity to legislate with the capacity to execute. It is contradictory that the sovereign, the *Gesetzgaber* (law-giver), also be the executer. They do not arise from the same phrase family: the former is an ideal of practical political reason, the latter the presentable referent of a cognitive phrase (from political sociology) that defines the domination of a master and says of him in the course of presenting him as the object validating this phrase: here is a case of it. As a function of this partition [*départage*], Kant thus concludes, or at least judges, that the form of domination that is the most propitious for a republic, because it is the most *repräsentativ*, is monarchy. We see that we must not be mistaken about the *Repräsentativität*, which is not at all a *Vorstellung*, but the name of a "passage" between two heterogeneous phrase families that serves to mark their heterogeneity, hence to maintain the abyss between them. I will let the reader be the judge whether this is the case for our contemporary modes of domination called democracies.

What can nonetheless be attributed to them in principle, as well as to the kind of monarchy Kant is thinking about, that of the century of Frederick the Great, is that their functioning is never devoid of deliberation, no matter where the instance of power is located. Now, if we inventory the phrase families put into play in deliberative political functioning, we cannot help but find again all the ones Kant isolates and mixes together in the historico-political writings. These are: the interro-prescriptive phrase: What must we do? (the determination of ends); the interro-descriptive phrase: What can we do? (the cognition of means, that is, the analysis of the data of experience); the imaginative phrase: here is what one could do (simulations, the elaboration of models); the antithetic phrase: the other is wrong, and here is why (debate); the rhetorical phrase: the other is wrong and I'm right, believe me (public polemics, opinion campaigns, propaganda); the adjudicative phrase: we decide about a given model that it gives the least bad response to the interro-prescriptive phrase (resolutions, programs, voting results); the prescriptive phrase: you must act in accordance with a given model (statutes, decrees, laws, circulars); the normative phrase: this prescription is legitimate (constitutional law); the judiciary phrase: such and such an action is not in conformity with the legitimate prescription (verdicts); the policing phrase: nonconforming action is subject to repression (coercion).

It seems to me that the "datum," which is really more of a *Begebenheit*, and which is this Center's business,[1] the *Begebenheit* that marks what has been called postmodernity to designate our time, is (if you allow me this symbol, though you *ought* to allow it to me) the feeling of a fissure in that great deliberative political core. As the *Begebenheit* that Kant confronted was occasioned by the French Revolution, the one that we, as philosophers and moral politicians, have to think about, and which is in no way homologous with the enthusiasm of 1789 (since it is not awoken by the Idea of an end, but by the Idea of several ends, or even by Ideas of heterogeneous ends), this *Begebenheit* of our time would thus lead into a new kind of sublime, one even more paradoxical than that of enthusiasm, in which not only the irremediable gap between an Idea and whatever presents itself in order to "realize" it would be felt, but also the gap between various phrase families and their respective legitimate presentations. The occasions for this highly cultivated "communitarian sense" would be called: Auschwitz, an abyss opened up when an object capable of validating the phrase of the Idea of human rights must be presented; Budapest 1956, an abyss opened up before the phrase of the Idea of the rights of peoples; Kolyma, an abyss opened up before the phrase of the (illusory) speculative concept of the dictatorship of the proletariat; 1968, an abyss opened up before the phrase of "democratic" illusion, which hid the heterogeneity between power and sovereignty. Each of these abysses, and others, should be explored in its difference and with precision. It remains that they all liberate judgment, at the same time that it is necessary to judge without criteria in order to feel them, and that this feeling in turn becomes a sign of history. But this political history must henceforth be judged *as if* it had made a further step in the direction of progress, that is to say, in the cultivation of skill and will. For it is not only the Idea of *an* end that is pointed out by our feeling, but already the Idea that this end consists in the formation and free exploration of Ideas, that this end is the beginning of the infinity of heterogeneous finalities. Everything that does not satisfy this fissuring of the end, everything that presents itself as the "realization" of a single end, which is the case with the phrase of *politics* [*la* politique], is felt not to be on the scale, *angemessen*, not "in affinity with" ["*en affine avec*"], *abgezielt*, the infinite capacity of the phrases that are delivered up in the feeling this fissuring arouses. And when I say, not commensurable, that's the least of it. This claim, we know, can be threatening to the point of embalming that which is nonetheless already dead, as in Red Square, or to bring a fable to life through terror and massacre, as under the Third Reich. Perpetual peace, but by the death of the capacity to judge.

Second word. The performative for which Philippe Lacoue-Labarthe and Jean-Luc Nancy turned out to be the empirical addressors—"A Center for philosophical research into the political is open"—was and is a phrase that opens a political field and a philosophical field. The field opened up is philosophical because the political is situated by this phrase as a referent to be signified throughout a series of phrases (those whose occurrences have been, are, and will be placed under the sign of this center, which is a region of the *Oeffentlichkeit* [public space]), and the phrases so solicited are phrases whose rules are not known and which aim not only to signify their referent (the political) but also on this occasion to signify their own rules. This is how they are philosophical in the sense of critical philosophy.

The field opened up by that inaugural performative is political just as well. The philosophical in effect (as a phrase whose aim is its rule) is situated by that performative as the genre of discourse or of concatenated phrases in which it is judged suitable to phrase the political, in preference to many other phrase families that also make claims to phrasing the political: the scientific (politicology), the narrative (history of political doctrines or political deeds), the epideictic (praising of the political), the juridical (public law), I could go on, without speaking of the stylistic or doctrinal variants within each of these, and of their concatenation into great discourses [*leur agencement en grands discours*]. By this presupposed suitability of the philosophical for the political, there is necessarily presupposed the principle whereby the political is not given (or no longer given) to be phrased as data that can be presented according to rules by phrases that are themselves regulated. However, and this too is part and parcel of the presupposition, the political nonetheless "delivers itself" ["*se livre*"]. This is the sense in which it was announced by Lacoue-Labarthe and Nancy as "prelogical." (I fear the *Schwärmerei* that clings to this word. "Parathetical" would be preferable.) Still, the Center's inaugural performative presupposes an event that affects the political and the philosophical and that undoubtedly affects the vigorous *Affekt* itself. This is what, in its indeterminacy, we must link up with. This presupposition is itself a political act.

Doesn't that something that would give rise to the political while effacing itself, which Lacoue-Labarthe and Nancy have suggested we call "*rapport*" [relation], and which they have ventured (erroneously, in my opinion) to designate by the name of "*Mère*" [Mother], bear some affinity with what, in following the Kantian labyrinth of "passages," I have symbolized as a "*mer*" [sea], the one in which the archipelago of phrases is dispersed, but also the one that leaves open the possibility of passages between them, uncertain ones, to be sure, and whose traces disappear to the point they must always trace over again, passages that to be sure are not bridges, but that can always be claimed since it is thanks to them that one phrase family finds in another the wherewithal to present the case on which it can be validated, in the likes of a sign, an example, a symbol, a type, a monogram, an ideal, and so on?

This sea is the linkage, both necessary and contingent: one cannot not link on, one has no preestablished rule by which to do it, but to establish the rule, one must link on. This linkage does not give rise to a system or a doctrine; it is the critical element.

And it links not only phrases but also their universes, and the addressors and addressees located therein. The "communitarian sense" of the third *Critique* is a designation of the linkage for heterogeneous addressors and addressees, in its necessity and contingency. The "retreat" of the political, which bears the names I've cited, unveils this element, but this element is itself always in retreat.

Final word. The idea of commensurability in the sense of an affinity without a rule that could serve as an established criteria, is decisive in Kantian thought, especially with regard to the historico-political. For us today, it strongly, all too strongly, tempers the event of fission. The explosion of language into families of heteronomous language games is the theme Wittgenstein, whether knowingly or not, gathers from Kant, and which he pursues as far as he can in the direction of rigorous description.[2] For the Kantian judge, it is not sufficient to decide one way or the other; it is necessary to sanction [*faire droit à*] the coexistence of what is heteronomous. The obligation to pass judgment presupposes an attraction, or a general interaction, between phrase families, despite their heteronomy, or because of it.

As for this urge toward commerce among phrases, Kant collapses its very Idea onto the Idea of a subject, which would otherwise shatter into pieces, onto the Idea of a reason, which would otherwise enter into conflict with itself and no longer merit its name. We today, and this is part and parcel of the *Begebenheit* of our time, feel that the fission it delivers also reaches into that subject and into that reason. Or at least, what there remains of attraction between the phrases of the postmodern Babel, what appears to verify them, at least within experience that is subject to concepts and direct presentations, is what we have, after Marx, learned to think as being that impostor of a subject and that blindly calculating reason called capital, in particular when it takes hold of phrases themselves to commercialize them and derive surplus value from them under the new conditions of *Gemeinwesen* known as the "information society." But as for the claim made by the phrase of capital to validate all phrases by its criterion of performativity, and the imposture that lifts capital into the place of the critical judge—there is, in the unnamed feeling that I have suggested making the *Begebenheit* of our time, the wherewithal to judge that claim and that imposture, to expose the elements of its critique and to reestablish within its rights the critical tribunal, which is nonetheless not the same as the criticist tribunal. It is not by the Idea of man and with a philosophy of the subject that we can judge them, but by the "passages" between heterogeneous phrases and with a respect for their heterogeneity. That is why a philosophy of phrases has more of an "affinity" with this *Begebenheit* than a philosophy of the faculties of a subject. But then, what can a critical tribunal be if the judge cannot regulate his judgments in terms of the Kantian ideal of the philosopher in the world, if he is incapable of believing that in judging he seeks to "favor the essential ends of human reason"?

To finish, I would formulate the direction (the guiding thread) that the *Begebenheit* delivered up by our time proposes to philosophy. Perhaps the ideal of reflection is not only, as Kant thought (in part against himself) to transform differends into litigations, to substitute the courtroom for the "battlefield" and for idioms. If it remains necessary to persist in the pursuit of this ideal, that would surely be without help from the Idea that nature pursues the end of human freedom through history, that is, without the help of the teleological hypothesis. Perhaps reflective responsibility today also consists in discerning, respecting, and making respected the differends, in establishing the incommensurability of the transcendental exigencies proper to heterogeneous phrase families, and to find other languages for what cannot be expressed within existing languages. That would be a way of being, without paradox, faithful to the Kantian Idea of "culture" understood as the trace of freedom within reality: culture is, writes Kant (*KUK* 299), "the aptitude to propose for oneself ends in general."

Notes

1. I analyze the public debates in the summer of 1983 over this sense of "abandonment" in my upcoming work, *The Retreat of the French Intellectual*.

NOTICE

1. [For details on the history and intellectual project of the Centre de recherches philosophiques sur le politique, see Simon Sparks's introduction to *Retreating the Political* (London: Routledge, 1997), xiv–xxviii. This volume also includes English translations of key texts written by Philippe Lacoue-Labarthe and Jean-Luc Nancy during the time they organized and ran the Center. For an earlier and less sympathetic assessment of the Center's activities, see Nancy Fraser, "The French Derrideans: Politicizing Deconstruction or Deconstructing the Political?" *New German Critique* 33 (autumn 1984): 127–54.—Trans.]

2. [A version of this "version" has been translated into English by Geoff Bennington as "The Sign of History," in *Post-Structuralism and the Question of History*, ed. Derek Attridge, Geoff Bennington, and Robert Young (Cambridge: Cambridge University Press, 1987), 162–80; rpt. *The Lyotard Reader*, ed. Andrew Benjamin (Oxford: Blackwell, 1989), 393–411.—Trans.]

3. [*Recherches sur la philosophie et le langage*. Cahier du Groupe de recherches sur la philosophie et le langage, no. 3 (Grenoble: Université des Sciences Sociales de Grenoble; Paris: Vrin, 1983), 107–28. As far as I am aware, no English translation of this "version" of Lyotard's study has ever been published.—Trans.]

4. *Le différend* was first published in Paris in 1983 by the Editions de Minuit. An English translation, *The Differend: Phrases in Dispute*, appeared in 1988 (Minneapolis: University of Minnesota Press).

5. [An English translation of Philippe Lacoue-Labarthe and Jean-Luc Nancy's "Opening Address to the Centre for Philosophical Research on the Political" can be found in *Retreating the Political*, ed. Simon Sparks, 107–21. The text in question by Nancy, "The Jurisdiction of the Hegelian Monarch," has been translated

by Mary Ann Caws and Peter Caws and appears in Jean-Luc Nancy, *The Birth to Presence* (Stanford: Stanford University Press, 1993), 110–42.—Trans.]

ARGUMENT

1. Immanuel Kant, *Critique of Pure Reason* (A: 1781; B: 1786) (hereafter, indicated as *KRV*), trans. Paul Guyer and Alan W. Wood (Cambridge: Cambridge University Press, 1998), 531. [Lyotard adds to this first Kant reference, the following remark: "All cited translations have been verified (against the German original) and sometimes modified." Later, in the first and fourth notes to Chapter 3, when introducing his analysis of Kant's smaller works on history and politics, he mentions that he "retranslates them according to the German text." This close attention to the words of the German original in relation to its French translation argues the need for the English translator to render as scrupulously as possible the particularity of the way Lyotard construes the Kantian text even as it more often than not diverges from the published English translations. I have followed this imperative throughout, so that generally speaking, *all* the citations from Kant in this translation should be understood as "modified." And while I have also consulted the vintage translations of Norman Kemp Smith, J. H. Bernard, Lewis White Beck, Robert Anchor, Mary Gregor, and others, I have most frequently relied, whenever possible, on the still-ongoing *Cambridge Edition of the Works of Immanuel Kant*, under the general editorship of Paul Guyer and Alan Wood, and the indicated pagination, unless otherwise noted, will refer to the Cambridge edition.—Trans.]

CHAPTER I

1. [On this debate between Jean-Luc Nancy and Luc Ferry, see Lyotard's Notice.—Trans.]

2. "Philosophy is the *system* of rational cognition through concepts, which already suffices to distinguish it from a critique of pure reason; since the latter contains a philosophical investigation of the possibility of such cognition, but does not belong to such a system as an integral part, from the very fact that it outlines and examines the very idea of it in the first place." [Immanuel Kant, *First Introduction to the Critique of the Power of Judgment (1789–1790)*, trans. Paul Guyer and Eric Matthews, in *Critique of the Power of Judgment* (Cambridge: Cambridge University Press, 2000), 3.]

3. Following the nomenclature of the introduction to the *Critique of the Power of Judgment* (1790) (hereafter, referred to as *KUK*), trans. Paul Guyer and Eric Matthews (Cambridge: Cambridge University Press, 2000), § II, 61–62f.

[The relevant paragraph in Kant reads as follows:

Concepts, insofar as they are related to objects, regardless of whether a cognition of the latter is possible or not, have their field, which is determined merely in accordance with the relation which their object has to our faculty of cognition in general.—The part of this field within which cognition is possible for us is a territory (*territorium*) for these concepts and the requisite faculty of cognition. The part of the territory in which these are legislative is the domain (*ditio*) of these concepts and of the corresponding faculty of cognition. Thus empirical concepts do indeed have their territory in nature, as the set of all objects of sense, but no domain (only their residence, *domicilium*); because they are, to be sure, lawfully generated, but are not legislative, rather the rules grounded on them are empirical, hence contingent.]

4. Jean-Luc Nancy, "Lapsus Judicii," *Communications* 26 (1977): 82 [An English translation by James Williams and David Webb appeared in *Pli: The Warwick Journal of Philosophy* 3, no. 2 (1991): 16–40.—Trans.] Rereading this remarkable article after the fact, I notice how much the present study is a humble cousin and everything this study owes to it, be it unconsciously. Centered like it is on the question of the *case* to be judged, this study differs in two aspects. On the one hand, in following the lessons of the second and third *Critiques* and of the historico-political studies, I extend the examination of the "this is the case" to presentations that, Kant avows, cannot be regulated either in the mode of examples or of schemata. On the other hand, I abstain from urging the modes and manners in the direction of "figuration" or "fictionalization" as Nancy does. It seems to me, having had recourse to them elsewhere, that these terms arise from a problematic of foundations and origins. Now, the emphasis Kant puts on judgment, perfectly well understood by Nancy, points to a reversal of the problematic of origins in favor of the question of ends, which Kant exposits under the name of Ideas. Considered in this fashion, the "as ifs" in their heterogeneity are not substituted for the ontological phrase whose synthesis would be lacking (*lapsus*), they are "passages" between "areas" [*aires*] of legitimacy (this is Nancy's word to say what I am here calling "islands" of legitimacy). For to grasp the Kantian "revolution" in its unannounced program, we need to get to the point of phrasing these "passages" otherwise than as substitutes [*suppléances*] aimed at conjugating the fragments of a dislocated origin, Being or subject. These passages, it seems to me, are already in Kant, language (which, if you like, is being without illusion) *in the course of* establishing various families of legitimacy— critical language, without rules to be sure, in the course of formulating the rules for various phrase games, including its own. This is where the Kantian problematic seems to me more "political" than juridical, or at least within the juridical to privilege the "political" over the judicial. But this divergence of opinion from Nancy's research can surely be resolved.

5. *KRV* 694–95. The definition of *Weltbegriffe* is found at the beginning of

the Antinomy of Pure Reason, *KRV* 460. The opposition *"für die Schule"/"aus der Schule in die Welt"* governs the article, "On the Common Saying; 'That May Be Correct in Theory, But It Is of No Use in Practice'" (1793); hereafter, indicated as *TP*, in Kant, *Practical Philosophy*, trans. and ed. by Mary J. Gregor (Cambridge: Cambridge University Press, 1996), 273.

6. The Idea of "the mathematical whole of all phenomena and the totality of their synthesis in the great as well as in the small" (*KRV*, "System of Cosmological Ideas," 465–66).

7. "This same world is called nature, insofar as it is considered a dynamic *whole*, and one does not look at the aggregation in space or time so as to bring about a quantity, but looks instead at the unity in *existence* of phenomena" (*KRV*). The world is nature when it is considered, as is the case in the third and fourth Antinomies, from the point of view of the dynamic absolute: absolute of causality (Antinomy of Freedom), absolute of the totality of conditions (Antinomy of the Supreme Being). What is introduced through the consideration of the *existence* of phenomena is the care to take stock of what remains of the datum once the scientific phrase has been formulated (Analytic). The Idea of dynamic nature in the *KRV* leads to the Idea of teleological nature in the *KUK*.

CHAPTER 2

1. *Critique of Practical Reason* (1788); hereafter, noted as *KPV*, trans. Mary J. Gregor, in *Practical Philosophy* (Cambridge: Cambridge University Press, 1996), 194ff.

2. Philippe Lacoue-Labarthe, "Typography," trans. Eduardo Cadava, in *Typography: Mimesis, Philosophy, Politics*, ed. Christopher Fynsk (Cambridge, MA: Harvard University Press, 1989), 43–138.

3. *KUK* § 70; *KUK* 258; *KUK* § 71, 261; *KUK* § 72, 261.

CHAPTER 3

1. See the critique of these three hypotheses in the *Conflict of the Philosophy Faculty with the Faculty of Law* (1797) (hereafter, referred to as *Conflict*), § III, French translation by Piobetta in Kant, *La philosophie de l'histoire (opuscules)* (Paris: Denoël, Bibliothèque Médiations, 1947), 165–67. [*The Conflict of the Faculties*, trans. Mary J. Gregor and Robert Anchor, in *Religion and Rational Theology* (Cambridge: Cambridge University Press, 1996), 299–300. All further references to this text will refer to the pagination in the Cambridge translation.—Trans.] Regarding the opuscules collected in Piobetta's edition, I will retranslate them in accordance with the German texts as found in the following: *Kleinere Schriften zur Geschichtsphilosophie, Ethik und Politik* (Hamburg:

Meiner, 1973); *Ausgewählte kleine Schriften* (Hamburg: Meiner, 1969); *Über den Gebrauch teleologischer Prinzipien in der Philosophie* (1788), in *Sämtliche Werke* (Leipzig: Meiner, 1922), VIII, 129–60; *Der Streit der philosophischen Fakultät mit der juristischen* (1797), in *Der Streit der Fakultäten* (Hamburg: Meiner, 1959. Cf. also *Le Conflit des Facultés*, trans. Gibelin, 3d ed. (Paris: Vrin, 1973). [Specific English references will be detailed when cited but are drawn from one of the following three volumes of the Cambridge edition: *Practical Philosophy* (1996), *Religion and Rational Theology* (1996), or *Anthropology, History, and Education* (2007).—Trans.]

2. *Idea for a Universal History from a Cosmopolitan Point of View* (1784) (hereafter, referred to as *Idea*), Sixth Thesis, trans. Allen W. Wood, in *Anthropology, History, and Education* (Cambridge: Cambridge University Press, 2007), 113.

3. *Remarks Concerning Observations on the Feeling of the Beautiful and the Sublime* [*Bemerkungen zu den Beobachtungen über das Gefühl des Schönen und Erhabenen*] (1764), in *Kant's gesammelte Schriften*, ed. Preußische Akademie der Wissenschaften (Berlin: Walter de Gruyter, 1942), XX, 88; cited this way by Georges Vlachos, *La pensée politique de Kant* (Paris: PUF, 1962), 92. Kant's text reads as follows: "Nothing is more awful for a man than having to subordinate his acts to the will of another. There is thus no more natural aversion for a man than that toward servitude. So it is that a child cries and gets upset when obliged to do what others want without their caring to know what he would like to do. His sole desire, then, is to become a man so as to dispose of his own affairs as he sees fit. [But] to get there, it is necessary that some servitude, emanating from things, takes form."

4. *TP*, passim; *Toward Perpetual Peace: A Philosophical Project* (1795) (hereafter, referred to as *Project*), Appendix I, trans. Mary J. Gregor, in *Practical Philosophy*, 338ff.; *Zum ewigen Frieden*, in *Kleiner Schriften zur Geschichtsphilosophie, Ethik und Politik*, op. cit.; *The Doctrine of Right* (1797), trans. Mary J. Gregor, in *Practical Philosophy*, § 49, Remark A, 461ff.; ibid., § 52, 480ff.; *Reflections* no. 7680, 8045, in *Kant's gesammelte Schriften*, ed. Preußische Akademie der Wissenschaften (Berlin: Walter de Gruyter, 1934), XIX, 486ff., 501; "Explanatory Remarks on the Metaphysical First Principles of the Doctrine of Right," conclusion, in *The Doctrine of Right*, 504ff.

5. Dating from 1788, in Kant, *Anthropology, History, and Education*, trans. Robert B. Louden, 195–98.

6. The "Cracow Fragment" ("Krakauer Fragment zum 'Streit der Fakultäten'") (1797?) calls it *"Ereignis."* Cf. Immanuel Kant, *Politische Schriften*, hgb von Otto Heinrich von der Gablentz (Köln und Opladen: Westdeutscher Verlag, 1965), 172. The first edition of the manuscript was procured by Klaus Weyand in *Kantstudien* 51 (1959–60), 1.

7. [See Alexandre Kojève, *Les peintures concrètes de Kandinsky* (Bruxelles: La Lettre volée, 2001).—Trans].

CHAPTER 4

1. *Proclamation of the Imminent Conclusion of a Treatise of Perpetual Peace in Philosophy* (1796) (hereafter, indicated as *Proclamation*), trans. Peter Heath in *Theoretical Philosophy After 1781* (Cambridge: Cambridge University Press, 2002), 453.

2. [There is a considerable variety of ways to translate the title of this essay: *Idee zu einer allgemeinen Geschichte in weltbürgerlicher Absicht*. In particular, the word "Absicht" can be rendered as "aim," "perspective," or "point of view," all with differing implications. Lyotard thus appears to be unique in his attention to the meaning of "weltbürgerlicher," typically translated as "cosmopolitan" (*cosmopolite* in standard French). Toward the end of Chapter 3 of this book, he interprets such a "cosmopolitan aim" as a kind of globalized civil society, to the extent that the expression, *bürgerlicher Gesellschaft*, refers to the concept of civil society within a particular sociopolitical entity, such as a nation-state. Such a reading of these Kant passages as heralding a kind of worldwide or globalized civil society would seem in turn to motivate his own translation of "*weltbügerlicher*" by "*cosmopolitique*," and it is in keeping with this rendering of the German expression to indicate a kind of transnational political civility (perhaps best concretized by the emergence and spread of NGO's) that I likewise have recourse to the neologism, "cosmopolitical."—Trans.]

3. *Answer to the Question: What Is Enlightenment?* (1784) (hereafter, noted as *Answer*), trans. Mary J. Gregor, *Practical Philosophy*, 18.

4. *Idea*, Fifth Proposition, 109; cf. also ibid., Second Proposition, 109–10; *KUK* § 83, 298; *Answer*, 20; *Conjectural Beginning of Human History* (1786) (hereafter, noted as *Conjecture*), trans. Allen W. Wood, in *Anthropolgy, History, and Education*, 167–68; ibid., 173.

CHAPTER 5

1. See Notice.

2. See Vincent Descombes's commentary on the Tugendhat books, "La philosophie comme science rigoureusement descriptive," *Critique* 407 (April 1981): 351–57.

Cultural Memory | *in the Present*

Sara Guyer, *Romanticism After Auschwitz*

Alison Ross, *The Aesthetic Paths of Philosophy: Presentation in Kant, Heidegger, Lacoue-Labarthe, and Nancy*

Gerhard Richter, *Thought-Images: Frankfurt School Writers' Reflections from Damaged Life*

Bella Brodzki, *Can These Bones Live? Translation, Survival, and Cultural Memory*

Rodolphe Gasché, *The Honor of Thinking: Critique, Theory, Philosophy*

Brigitte Peucker, *The Material Image: Art and the Real in Film*

Natalie Melas, *All the Difference in the World: Postcoloniality and the Ends of Comparison*

Jonathan Culler, *The Literary in Theory*

Michael G. Levine, *The Belated Witness: Literature, Testimony, and the Question of Holocaust Survival*

Jennifer A. Jordan, *Structures of Memory: Understanding German Change in Berlin and Beyond*

Christoph Menke, *Reflections of Equality*

Marlène Zarader, *The Unthought Debt: Heidegger and the Hebraic Heritage*

Jan Assmann, *Religion and Cultural Memory: Ten Studies*

David Scott and Charles Hirschkind, *Powers of the Secular Modern: Talal Asad and His Interlocutors*

Gyanendra Pandey, *Routine Violence: Nations, Fragments, Histories*

James Siegel, *Naming the Witch*

J. M. Bernstein, *Against Voluptuous Bodies: Late Modernism and the Meaning of Painting*

Theodore W. Jennings, Jr., *Reading Derrida / Thinking Paul: On Justice*

Richard Rorty and Eduardo Mendieta, *Take Care of Freedom and Truth Will Take Care of Itself: Interviews with Richard Rorty*

Jacques Derrida, *Paper Machine*

Renaud Barbaras, *Desire and Distance: Introduction to a Phenomenology of Perception*

Jill Bennett, *Empathic Vision: Affect, Trauma, and Contemporary Art*

Ban Wang, *Illuminations from the Past: Trauma, Memory, and History in Modern China*

James Phillips, *Heidegger's Volk: Between National Socialism and Poetry*

Frank Ankersmit, *Sublime Historical Experience*

István Rév, *Retroactive Justice: Prehistory of Post-Communism*

Paola Marrati, *Genesis and Trace: Derrida Reading Husserl and Heidegger*

Krzysztof Ziarek, *The Force of Art*

Marie-José Mondzain, *Image, Icon, Economy: The Byzantine Origins of the Contemporary Imaginary*

Cecilia Sjöholm, *The Antigone Complex: Ethics and the Invention of Feminine Desire*

Jacques Derrida and Elisabeth Roudinesco, *For What Tomorrow . . . : A Dialogue*

Elisabeth Weber, *Questioning Judaism: Interviews by Elisabeth Weber*

Jacques Derrida and Catherine Malabou, *Counterpath: Traveling with Jacques Derrida*

Martin Seel, *Aesthetics of Appearing*

Nanette Salomon, *Shifting Priorities: Gender and Genre in Seventeenth-Century Dutch Painting*

Jacob Taubes, *The Political Theology of Paul*

Jean-Luc Marion, *The Crossing of the Visible*

Eric Michaud, *An Art for Eternity: The Cult of Art in Nazi Germany*

Anne Freadman, *The Machinery of Talk: Charles Peirce and the Sign Hypothesis*

Stanley Cavell, *Emerson's Transcendental Etudes*

Stuart McLean, *The Event and Its Terrors: Ireland, Famine, Modernity*

Beate Rössler, ed., *Privacies: Philosophical Evaluations*

Bernard Faure, *Double Exposure: Cutting Across Buddhist and Western Discourses*

Alessia Ricciardi, *The Ends of Mourning: Psychoanalysis, Literature, Film*

Alain Badiou, *Saint Paul: The Foundation of Universalism*

Gil Anidjar, *The Jew, The Arab: A History of the Enemy*

Jonathan Culler and Kevin Lamb, eds., *Just Being Difficult? Academic Writing in the Public Arena*

Jean-Luc Nancy, *A Finite Thinking*, edited by Simon Sparks

Theodor W. Adorno, *Can One Live after Auschwitz? A Philosophical Reader*, edited by Rolf Tiedemann

Patricia Pisters, *The Matrix of Visual Culture: Working with Deleuze in Film Theory*

Talal Asad, *Formations of the Secular: Christianity, Islam, Modernity*

Dorothea von Mücke, *The Rise of the Fantastic Tale*

Marc Redfield, *The Politics of Aesthetics: Nationalism, Gender, Romanticism*

Emmanuel Levinas, *On Escape*

Dan Zahavi, *Husserl's Phenomenology*

Rodolphe Gasché, *The Idea of Form: Rethinking Kant's Aesthetics*

Michael Naas, *Taking on the Tradition: Jacques Derrida and the Legacies of Deconstruction*

Herlinde Pauer-Studer, ed., *Constructions of Practical Reason: Interviews on Moral and Political Philosophy*

Jean-Luc Marion, *Being Given: Toward a Phenomenology of Givenness*

Theodor W. Adorno and Max Horkheimer, *Dialectic of Enlightenment*

Ian Balfour, *The Rhetoric of Romantic Prophecy*

Martin Stokhof, *World and Life as One: Ethics and Ontology in Wittgenstein's Early Thought*

Gianni Vattimo, *Nietzsche: An Introduction*

Jacques Derrida, *Negotiations: Interventions and Interviews, 1971–1998*, edited by Elizabeth Rottenberg

Brett Levinson, *The Ends of Literature: Post-transition and Neoliberalism in the Wake of the "Boom"*

Timothy J. Reiss, *Against Autonomy: Global Dialectics of Cultural Exchange*

Hent de Vries and Samuel Weber, eds., *Religion and Media*

Niklas Luhmann, *Theories of Distinction: Redescribing the Descriptions of Modernity*, ed. and introd. William Rasch

Johannes Fabian, *Anthropology with an Attitude: Critical Essays*

Michel Henry, *I Am the Truth: Toward a Philosophy of Christianity*

Gil Anidjar, *"Our Place in Al-Andalus": Kabbalah, Philosophy, Literature in Arab-Jewish Letters*

Hélène Cixous and Jacques Derrida, *Veils*

F. R. Ankersmit, *Historical Representation*

F. R. Ankersmit, *Political Representation*

Elissa Marder, *Dead Time: Temporal Disorders in the Wake of Modernity (Baudelaire and Flaubert)*

Reinhart Koselleck, *The Practice of Conceptual History: Timing History, Spacing Concepts*

Niklas Luhmann, *The Reality of the Mass Media*

Hubert Damisch, *A Childhood Memory by Piero della Francesca*

Hubert Damisch, *A Theory of /Cloud/: Toward a History of Painting*

Jean-Luc Nancy, *The Speculative Remark (One of Hegel's Bons Mots)*

Jean-François Lyotard, *Soundproof Room: Malraux's Anti-Aesthetics*

Jan Patočka, *Plato and Europe*

Hubert Damisch, *Skyline: The Narcissistic City*

Isabel Hoving, *In Praise of New Travelers: Reading Caribbean Migrant Women Writers*

Richard Rand, ed., *Futures: Of Derrida*

William Rasch, *Niklas Luhmann's Modernity: The Paradox of System Differentiation*

Jacques Derrida and Anne Dufourmantelle, *Of Hospitality*

Jean-François Lyotard, *The Confession of Augustine*

Kaja Silverman, *World Spectators*

Samuel Weber, *Institution and Interpretation: Expanded Edition*

Jeffrey S. Librett, *The Rhetoric of Cultural Dialogue: Jews and Germans in the Epoch of Emancipation*

Ulrich Baer, *Remnants of Song: Trauma and the Experience of Modernity in Charles Baudelaire and Paul Celan*

Samuel C. Wheeler III, *Deconstruction as Analytic Philosophy*

David S. Ferris, *Silent Urns: Romanticism, Hellenism, Modernity*

Rodolphe Gasché, *Of Minimal Things: Studies on the Notion of Relation*

Sarah Winter, *Freud and the Institution of Psychoanalytic Knowledge*

Samuel Weber, *The Legend of Freud: Expanded Edition*

Aris Fioretos, ed., *The Solid Letter: Readings of Friedrich Hölderlin*

J. Hillis Miller / Manuel Asensi, *Black Holes / J. Hillis Miller; or, Boustrophedonic Reading*

Miryam Sas, *Fault Lines: Cultural Memory and Japanese Surrealism*

Peter Schwenger, *Fantasm and Fiction: On Textual Envisioning*

Didier Maleuvre, *Museum Memories: History, Technology, Art*

Jacques Derrida, *Monolingualism of the Other; or, The Prosthesis of Origin*

Andrew Baruch Wachtel, *Making a Nation, Breaking a Nation: Literature and Cultural Politics in Yugoslavia*

Niklas Luhmann, *Love as Passion: The Codification of Intimacy*

Mieke Bal, ed., *The Practice of Cultural Analysis: Exposing Interdisciplinary Interpretation*

Jacques Derrida and Gianni Vattimo, eds., *Religion*